# A Note to the Reader

Hello, my name is Carlos, I'm not a writer nor do I have any idea how to write or publish a book. I don't seek fame or to show off, I only wish to inform others of my life story with the desire to help those who suffer, who seek a will to survive.

In this story you will find a real and true orientation in which you can confide in to help cease your frustrations, limitations and anxieties.

I have poured all of my passion, dedication and enthusiasm into this book to give you my life testimony, hoping to motivate you and fill you with the strength to face adversity. Here you will find a relentless struggle, seeking to surpass all limits and obstacles in your journey to reach your personal, professional, emotional, and spiritual goals. In my words there is a great outpouring of faith and enthusiasm.

My wish is that the light and brightness would dispel the darkness in your life.

Thank you for accepting this book that will in a way minimize your sorrows and pains.

Also, thank you to all my beloved friends and family in the whole world for their prayers and unconditional support, the reason I'm still alive.

Carlos Patiño Effio

# Author's Biography

## CARLOS PATIÑO EFFIO

He was born on October 7, 1952 in the district of Rimac, Lima, Peru.

He worked for more than eighteen years in the Central Mortgage Bank of Peru, and among other important positions, he served as Head of Personnel Management, Head of Asset Control, Head of Legal Interventions, General Subsecretary of the Board and Supervisor of Branches and Agencies.

In 1981 he attended as a delegate of Peru to the "IX International Congress of Personnel Management" (CIAP) in Viña del Mar, Chile.

While working in Lima, at the Central Mortgage Bank of Peru, in 1982 he reorganized the system of the Archives of the Bank in an agreement made with the General Archive of the Nation of Peru.

In 1997, residing in the United States of America, he spent six years as manager of major restaurants in Miami Florida.

In 2003 he came to North Carolina where he currently resides and works at Members Credit Union, a non-profit institution, since July 2004. He served as Director of Latino Services since December 2005 until September 2012. In October of that same year he was promoted to Vice President of Latino Services.

In 2005 he became Director of Centro Latino "Spanish Action" in Winston-Salem, North Carolina.

In 2008 he participated as a committee member of Public Relations in "The Arts Council" of Winston-Salem.

He was recognized as the "Latino Leader of 2011", receiving the Hanesbrands, Inc. award in recognition for his constant work in support of the noble and strongly dedicated Hispanic community of Winston-Salem/Forsyth County, during the prestigious "Spanish Nite" ceremony organized by the Hispanic League.

In April 2012 he was recognized by the Winston Lake Family YMCA for his contribution to the financial education of the Latino community through the program "Latino Achievers".

During his work at Members Credit Union he accomplished the following achievements:

• Substantially increased the presence of Latino members.

• In 2008 he presented the project for the creation of the Kernersville branch, the Members Credit Union's first Spanish branch, which was approved and inaugurated the same year.

• In 2010 created the "Latino Museum", the first Latino museum established in an office, collecting more than 400 valuable objects from all Latin American countries, which was inaugurated May 5th of the same year. This project was strongly supported by all his friends, among them the members. In June 2011 he was recognized for this distinguished work on the front page of the important local paper "Winston-Salem Journal".

Carlos constantly appears in interviews in major local and out-of-state newspapers, as well as on local radio and educational TV channels in Winston-Salem. He has also been interviewed for multi-media communications of Lima, Peru.

Carlos is a great bulwark of the Latino community and strongly supports non-profit organizations to achieve their internal objectives.

Carlos Patiño Effio

PASSION FOR LIFE…
A message to the willpower

Prologue by
Martín Balarezo García

Printed by
CreateSpace
Member of the Amazon Group

Edited by
Martín Balarezo García
martinbalarezogarcia@live.com

Translated by
Andrea Balarezo Bachmann

Cover design by
César Herbas
cesarherbas@live.com

CreateSpace

PASSION FOR LIFE...
A message to the willpower

Copyright © 2012 by Carlos Patiño Effio
All rights reserved
First edition: October 7, 2012

Library of Congress Control Number: 2012916862
ISBN: 978-0-615-69708-6

PRINTED IN THE UNITED STATES OF AMERICA

# *Dedication*

In memory of Marianella,
my daughter..., "my great inspiration".

# Acknowledgements

In the beautiful memory of my dear father Pedro "Cucho" and my brother Pedro the "Nono" who now live next to God.

Saluting the courage and bravery of my mother Vilma, who, despite many years of being disabled, remains strong and steadfast in her struggle for life.

To Sebastiana, my "Nana", for the 60 years of dedication to our family with love and generosity.

To my brothers Walter and Manuel, for their generous support during difficult times.

To my beloved sons Carlos Alfonso and Juan Carlos, who give me their love and understanding every day.

Finally, to my grandson Nicholas, the treasure and joy of my life.

The author

X

# *Prologue*

There may be many special moments in life, but few are the transcendental, one of them came at the beginning of this year when I was fortunate enough to meet Carlos Patiño Effio from afar. Our mutual and appreciated friend, Harold Jahnsen, allowed us to get in contact and opened my world to this monumental work that I present with great pride and pleasure.

"PASSION FOR LIFE... A message to the willpower" is a book that not only contains intense and heartbreaking words, it also a story full of sincerity and noble sentiments, a passionate and hopeful story, an anthem to life and willpower.

Virginia, September 12, 2012

Martín Balarezo García

# *Index*

# INTRODUCTION

This is a story of almost twenty-eight years of hardship, terrible sadness, suffering and ailment. Of all of these years, five were spent watching my daughter slowly die, held captive by a terrible disease, and the last fifteen years are my account of an intense, desperate, permanent and constant struggle to beat cancer, the horrible disease, which in its different forms kills millions of people around the world. With this battle it is fifteen times that I'm fighting to save my life, trying to survive this terrible, painful, cruel, difficult and sometimes misunderstood disease. My joy, my enthusiasm and, above all, my faith in God and in myself are my best allies. Also, my fight to create a path, rise up, progress and become someone in life make up my greatest inspirations.

I thank God for letting me live and tell my story. I hope to live to see how this book will benefit and help all those in need of a sincere, profound, direct, and accurate message to their "WILLPOWER" to continue confronting their problems in a completely different way.

This book is intended for all those who are walking through life, some enjoying good health and others sick, either physically or spiritually. In many cases, economic wealth can't restore health much less help find inner peace. It takes more than money to save a life and to live in peace and harmony. It requires the use of something else, something special and powerful, the use of "OUR OWN INNER STRENGTH" that the Supreme Being has given us all without exception. The important thing is recognizing that "YES YOU CAN ACHIEVE ANYTHING YOU DESIRE".

In this book you will find a real life story. My intention is that this book will somehow provide guidance and direction to address the ailments of body and soul. I will explain how I fight to establish a relationship between body, mind and energy and how I face life even when

I sometimes feel I've lost its meaning and my desire to keep fighting.

Through my story you will know how to face your fears, weakness, shame, hatred, resentment and other impairments that are the negative part of your body and can lead to the end of your existence.

I also describe how to direct boundless enthusiasm into a tired body, very mistreated yet eager to live and how to deal with the situation with determination, willpower and always hand in hand with a "BIG SMILE".

Also, you'll be able to see the difference between yourself, a special person with great enthusiasm and drive to live and fight to achieve your most cherished desires despite all of your problems and difficulties, with others who do not appreciate what they have and just complain and regret all the time. These people are full of "social barriers" that limit them and lock them into their own prison, a prison of the mind and soul where people are full of complexes and are creators of their own misfortune and misery. These people prefer to consult their mirror expecting to receive only the answers they want to hear, without focusing on the splendor of their own "POWERFUL AND IMMEASURABLE WILLPOWER" to overcome all of their problems.

Those who feel less than others and are terrified with life are people unable to do more for themselves. They feel insecure and prefer to take advantage of a series of excuses instead of trying things out, just to avoid mistakes, but they are the first to criticize the "daring" ones who do mess up and mess up many times in their bold attempts to reach their goals. Those "brave" ones are the ones who learn from their mistakes and failures during the process of achieving their dreams and are enriched with all that precious experience they gain every day on their journey down the "ROAD TO SUCCESS".

This life story has not been written to cause mourning, although in many of its pages there is profound and marked pain. Here is an extraordinary and sincere message of "STRENGTH and LOVE" for what you are...: "a chosen being" worthy and capable of doing what you want for yourself. I give you an outpouring of joy, enthusiasm, determination and above all, a "WILL TO LIVE", written directly for you and whoever else wishes to take advantage of it.

Nobody has told me this story, I have not read about it, it is not part of another book or story, much less is it a fictional piece to evoke your emotions. I've been living and suffering through this every day for almost twenty-eight years.

This book is something different. Written in my own style, it breaks the traditional, conservative approach to writing a book; it looks to do what I love, to "innovate". Times have changed and we need something different where people can identify with circumstances like their own, not on fictional models created only for "commercial purposes". It is aimed toward the people of all social levels, economic and educational with the goal to achieve a better and easier understanding of what is further explained. It is dedicated to all those people wanting to forever leave behind their health problems and social limitations, and who want to be free of restrictions in order to excel and make progress in life.

Social barriers are like a wall that doesn't let you move ahead; it traps you, pressures you, and doesn't let you develop "YOUR TALENT AND ABILITY". The best of yourself is postponed, hidden and left behind. Do not let anything or anyone make you feel less of yourself. Humility is a virtue, but never allow yourself to be humiliated; being humiliated is a moral attack. Also, social discrimination is an assault toward your human rights... DO NOT LET THIS HAPPEN! Declare yourself a free person; declare yourself a being of equal social status with the same rights and responsibilities as everyone else. You're not lacking anything. Haven't you noticed many people with disabilities striving to live a normal life, competing and fighting against their own limitations to achieve their goals? Make a decision to be different..., TO BE BETTER EVERY DAY!

Finally, if you are one of those people who loves hurting yourself and looking for a way to make your life miserable, stabbing yourself with your own "little knives" in order to feel pain, anger, pessimism, cowardice, resentment and believe to be less than others, giving life no chance and even regretting the day you were born, looking for excuses about why it can't be done, then do not read this book.

This book is dedicated to those who want to rise to another level in life and to excel; to those, who like the "Phoenix" bird of Greek mythology that emerged victorious from the flames, ashes and rubble, can push off and rise above their troubles, difficulties and limitations, filling their lives with a lot of love, strength, joy, energy, enthusiasm, faith, and mental, social, moral and professional development. The most important thing is to seek and accept change and become free and healthy, full of inner peace and the ability to look into the future, but toward a different future..., "A BETTER FUTURE".

Nothing is impossible to achieve... "IT ONLY DEPENDS ON YOU".

The author

# PART I

# MY STORY

# CHAPTER I
## HOW MY STORY BEGINS...

It was July of 1997 when I left Lima, Peru, toward the city of Miami, Florida, in the United States of America. I came to this country carrying a suitcase full of regrets, failures, distress, anxiety, desolation, sadness, frustration, pain, fear, bitterness, despair and insecurity. It was a heavy load and a great burden and pressure lay on my shoulders for the immense responsibility of my future and that of my children. At the same time, that suitcase was full of rebellion, courage, willpower, valor, love of life and "guts", ready and determined to strive to face every challenge and eager to get ahead of that terrifying moral anguish and despair, thinking that it might be the last chance life would give me, "amusingly or mockingly", to test if I could guide my future and my family. I never imagined the high cost I would pay for such a bold challenge. It would be a very expensive price. I also didn't think it would be 15 years before I would be able to return to my country.

Upon arriving to Miami, I felt totally alone, away from all of my family, like an abandoned child, frightened, not knowing where to go or where to start; all I had was the solace of holding on to the undershirt I had on that had been stamped with a picture of my children and their nicknames, "Foncho" y "Juanca". They got me the shirt before I traveled, sacrificing part of the little money I left for them while I got settled down in a new country, a shirt that I still own after 15 years for the intrinsic value that it holds for me. They stayed under the care of their mother.

My few relatives in Miami could not help me at all, neither at the time of my arrival, when I had nowhere to go, and much less with my illness. I understand and respect the fact that maybe they thought I would be a large burden for them.

Thank God a good friend answered my desperate calls from the airport where I felt lost. He was kind enough to "rescue" me and leave me at the house of some "friends". I spent two nights sleeping in a broken car, with the Miami heat and mosquitoes that would not let me even close my eyes. What a welcome..., right?! I couldn't let myself use the little money I had brought from Peru to start my life in this country. I became completely distressed, full of immense pain for being separated from the most precious things to me, Carlos Alfonso "Foncho" almost 16 years old, and Juan Carlos "Juanca" 10 years old, my children, my adorations, my reasons for living, everything I had and all I have, whom I feel very proud of. We had never been separated. Before leaving I promised that we would meet again soon, but not in Lima.

My sadness came from seeing them so young facing the separation from their father. It worried me and made me feel uneasy knowing that they needed me as father and friend. It also hurt me watching them suffer the pain from the divorce of their parents, which was disastrous and disturbing for all of us.

Through the window of the plane, landing in Miami, I saw a large, majestic and magnificent city. It was both impressive and disturbing. I felt a combination of fear, insecurity and a great sorrow, because I came to face life in complete confusion, worried, with my mind ready to burst of chaos and with great emptiness inside. I had left behind the greatest thing for me, my children, and felt the rending from the inconsolable loss of my daughter Marianella who was 6 years old. She died after a long and grueling battle against a disease that had her prostrate and hopeless and just waiting for the last moment of her existence.

Those were the hardest, most painful and frightening five years of my life that at the end not only left me bitter and destroyed, but also drowning in anguish and the fear of being unable to share it with friends and family for comfort and support because of the damaged social order at that time. Similarly, the despair of seeing my kids who were involved and engaged in this terrible and distressing situation took possession over me. They were not guilty of anything. Life was being cruel and disastrous to my family and me.

Many people suffer the pain of burying a father, mother, brother or a close relative, but it is so hard having to see the life of your child end, having to bury her and dispel the illusion and hope of a life engendered by you. Especially when this misfortune is due to a slow and long illness, which has no cure.

"Mary", as we affectionately called Marianella, died at age 6, a victim of AIDS, that terrible and vicious disease that lashed furiously at the time.

The torture of the social condemnation toward my children, along with the ignorance, misunderstanding and heartbreaking looks that could make you feel like a wretched being were like an accusing finger pointed at your face. Sharp eyes pierced me mercilessly and accused me that I could also be "infected" and that somehow I could be the transmitter of the infection for others. I saw how people, smiling nervously, showed fear, worry and discomfort with our presence, which was my greatest anguish, despair and sadness. That was like slow and painful agony.

No one can have the slightest idea or even begin to imagine what I went through and what I felt inside as a human being and more so as a parent. The feeling of terror came over me at the possibility of losing my other children, whether by that terrible and cruel disease or any other cruel life incident. I was tortured, terrorized and suffering daily by the impotence of feeling branded for life and because maybe my descendants would not have a future. Each time one of them was sick, immediately the thought that it could be the sickness that took Mary's life came to mind, and I would feel frightened to have to go through that same calamity once again. I felt terrified of having to see them suffer with no cure. I found myself ruthlessly and brutally hurt. I wished to die but was not entitled to that because I had two small children looking to their father as their only support and hope. I was left damaged, mistreated, with no end in sight.

I still remember the December holidays, seeing the overflowing joy of people at Christmas and also the enthusiasm of the people heading to celebrate the New Year. I would spend it with Mary in my arms watching the happiness of other people through the living room window of my apartment in the district of San Isidro, as I felt the most appalling and terrible disappointment and bitterness in my heart and in deepest recesses of my soul for what I was living with her. I felt out of this world, lost, devastated, distraught and extremely sad.

During Mary's illness, I looked for a trustworthy, sensitive, warm doctor who would help us and who wouldn't "report" us. Finally my cousins through marriage, doctors in different fields, husbands of my first cousins, did what they could to help. The first one was there in the beginning and the second, a colonel in the Peruvian air force, accompanied me until the end.

Initially, with the suspicion of the disease, the hospital where we went recommended that we admit her, which I did not accept for fear that she would become just an experiment, since we knew that there was nothing to do to save her life. Because of this, I made the decision to give up everything of mine to stay with her and help her to the end.

At that time it was difficult to see AIDS in children because it was still somewhat new to medicine and especially because there was not a lot known about the disease, its origin and its sources of infection. They spoke that it was spread through sexual intercourse, and then later attributed it to groups of people with different sexual orientation and other such reasons. In short, diverse theories, but to see the disease in children was far too difficult to understand. Why let the indifference of medical science only subject both her and us to greater suffering?

What was happening to Mary was not fair from any point of view. Seeing a child suffer is the most terrible thing there is. I, as a parent, was and am willing to do whatever it takes to prevent the suffering of my children.

I was determined to carry out my promise of being by her side to take care of her, protect her, and accompany her through her condition until the end of her days. It was heartbreaking to watch her suffer and try to understand what was happening to her. Actually I find it hard to recount each moment spent with her, there are so many, it would be a form of morbidity or sadism to relive and bring to mind all those awful moments and days. I can only say that the disease was destroying her every day, exhausting and depleting her strength and her desire to play and be a child. I lived every day of my life with the anguish of knowing that I could do nothing to help.

Among many things, I remember one of those terrible nights when Mary came to my bed with intense itching all over her body. I gently helped her scratch but in my deep physical and mental fatigue I begged not to fall asleep before she did.

Mary was paying for human error with her life. She was a happy child and always demonstrated her valor. Yet sometimes she said she knew she would die.

Life at home was very difficult in every way, both in terms of family and marriage. Foncho and Juan Carlos were children, they wanted to play, go outside, and attend children's parties and different events for their age group. Mary needed a lot of care and especially a lot of understanding, love, patience and commitment. I did my best to try to please everyone.

After much suffering, as her lungs could take no more, Mary's life finally ended on the sad night of May 13, 1990. After her passing, we felt the chill of deep emptiness she left behind. The terrible and immense pain of her absence seized us on her birthday two months after her departure. The Christmas after her death was indescribable, full of bitterness and pain in her memory.

How courageous Mary was!... I still think about her suffering and yet her desire to live. Can you imagine how incomprehensible it is to see the life of someone so little end? A heart murmur was the beginning of the end. The options to cure her disease were to go to Spain, USA or Brazil. The three countries, I was told, had great experience in dealing with heart problems. I thought that Brazil was the most convenient because of its proximity and language that was not so difficult to understand. That choice was an immense and grave error, the error with which her death sentence was signed, because everything indicated that my daughter was infected with the AIDS virus through blood transfusions. With that, all of Marianella's hope for life was destroyed. It has been almost twenty-eight years since she was infected, but the moral damage that undermined our visions of seeing her grow up happy, healthy, full of life, with a great future ahead of her and bringing all that beautiful spirituality and wonderful happiness that girls bestow to a family, will never be compensated.

My wife and I arrived in the city of Sao Paulo with Foncho, 3 years old, whom I did not leave for fear that he would feel abandoned upon one day waking up and seeing that both his parents and Marianella were gone. I felt that I was somehow betraying him. I did not want him to feel that the family unit was broken. My goal has always been and will continue to be to respect my children's feelings, no matter how small they may be.

All children deserve love, respect, understanding, support, affection and warmth. Why wait until they are sick or have other problems to be interested and involved in the "BEAUTIFUL AND WONDERFUL WORLD OF CHILDHOOD"? There is nothing more beautiful than the joy they transmit through a laugh, or to see a cute and innocent smile on their face. They, in my personal opinion, need to be able to play openly, so that they don't develop certain complexes and limitations during their stage of growth. Many times I have heard some said: "don't get your clothes dirty", "don't play with the water, you'll catch a cold", "don't play with the dirt", "don't walk barefoot", "don't jump on that, you might get hurt", "don't run, you might fall", "take care of your toys", "take care of your shoes", "behave yourself", "don't do this", "don't do that", etc. It shouldn't be like that, let children realize these things in the most natural way. Let them get dirty, let them play with water or dirt, let them jump, run and break their toys. Why limit them, why create obstacles during childhood that will damage their future? Let them be what they are: children. They need to be in touch with nature so that their true personalities can blossom. Of course everything has its limits. Actually, allowing them to explore more freely will allow one to observe any negative behavior in their development and act upon or correct any problem that arises. It is very sad to see a child in a wheelchair or crutches, wanting to play and have fun, and the parents wishing they could see their child happy.

If your children are healthy then let them be happy, in fact, play with them, participate in their "antics" and enjoy those beautiful and unique moments in their growth that will never come back. And if unfortunately they do not already, help them to feel equal to other small ones. Children are the best example to follow. You can see them sick, but still they draw the strength to push forward.

Sometimes children can surprise us with their "FAITH IN THEMSELVES" and their tremendous desire to overcome all of their disabilities, which often, even adults cannot do. I am a fervent advocate for children. I do not support or believe in libertinism. I support well-directed rules and discipline, both enforced with "UNDERSTANDING AND

LOVE". They can understand everything, many times more than we do, they are very wise, we just need to take the time necessary to speak to them and let them know the way things are. Nothing is achieved through violence! That is a brutal, savage, and abnormal crime. Erase the word "punishment" from your mind and trade it for love, support, warmth, understanding, and guidance in their behavior. Do not sow fear but sow confidence. That way you will you always be with them, watching them grow up healthy, full of life, happy and consequently with a great future. It's not enough to say "here you do what I say because I say it and that's final". That's an abusive way to treat a child. They are our world's future and what we all want is a different and just world. Growing up healthy and free from all bondage they can accomplish it... "The smile of a child illuminates, determines and enriches the future of our world".

When we arrived at Sao Paulo, we moved into the home of Mrs. Maria, a big-hearted Brazilian lady. She was devoted to providing board and lodging to the people who came to the city with these types of heart problems. She always exhibited signs of altruism, showing us concern, love, affection, friendship and solidarity towards us and towards all who lived there. Her cooking was delicious. It was a house with a good living environment, where you could feel confidence and security. There we met other families from different countries with the same health problems. I remember there was a beautiful little Uruguayan girl with heart problems, who was considered a "blue-blood girl". After leaving Brazil we didn't hear any more about them or their fate.

I always wondered how Mary could have gotten infected. What was it that happened? Who was responsible for that tragedy? That mistake caused my daughter's death and brought upon us immense, excessive, and extreme pain.

Sometimes, medicine causes severe pain with its mistakes, causing disappointment and distrust. I firmly believe that there are many doctors who love their profession, true professionals who pour all of their dedication, love and determination into saving a life. I also believe that this supreme effort, along with a little more compassion would have a greater impact on the cure of diseases. Death creates much suffering, especially when it comes to children. They leave great sadness in their parents' hearts and a void that is impossible to fill. It is an open wound that will never close.

My mind is filled with memories of every day that Mary was in the Sao Paulo hospital. The moment we had to give her to the hospital to start her treatment was very painful. I felt extremely sad leaving her scared and crying. It was something terrible. When I got to the boarding house where we lived, I could not talk to the others who lived there because my eyes overflowed with tears at the slightest word. I thought about how she must feel, alone with no one she knew nearby. Every night, before leaving the hospital, I would make every effort to put her to sleep so that she wouldn't suffer watching us leave. The hospital wouldn't allow us to stay overnight with her. Twenty-eight years ago, everything was different.

My suffering has been so great throughout my life, and by witnessing the immense pain my daughter, Mary had to go through during so many sad and rending moments, that I truly learned what it was to have "SOUL PAIN". To me, soul pain means the worst pain a human is able to withstand. It enters and hits the inside of your body violently, it penetrates and pierces your gut and goes directly into your soul. It's an extremely strong pain that finally leaves a deep scar on the inside, a scar that is impossible to erase.

Mary was born on July 18, 1983, the day when the Catholic world celebrates "The Day of our Lady Fatima", and the sad and devastating day that she died coincidentally was the day my country was celebrating "Mother's Day". I felt anguished, like a complete failure, very demoralized and worn. I was lost, confused, and full of fear and insecurities. I was no longer the same and I never would be again.

Arriving in the United States was a very abrupt and frustrating change for me. I felt alone, in a big new city for me, different, with a language I did not speak. My goal was completely focused on finding an immediate and urgent solution to my terrible problems. I had left behind a country with no opportunities, much less for a 45 year old like me. Everything was against me and I didn't have a clear path to follow. My mind was like a broken film machine, at all times replaying the movie of my shattered life. The memories constantly hit my mind. I wondered how to turn back time and prevent the disaster and misfortune from ever having knocked on the door of my heart and my emotions.

That fateful night, in the moments that Mary's life was ending, my son Foncho awoke, amid the screams of his mother, and was horrified to see so much anguish and pain.

During his sister's funeral, my son's biggest concern was whether there was a spider in her coffin. I saw all our friends come to the funeral wake trying to comfort us for our misfortune. My mind was racing at a hundred miles per hour uncontrollable and almost deranged. At one point, while I observed my beloved "Fonchito" I remembered the day when we had to take him to a local clinic because of an infection he got on his fingers. The doctor had to make a small incision to relieve the problem and Mary cried inconsolably watching her brother go through that pain. Those were terribly disastrous, sad and chaotic moments. Many experiences, which are now only memories, come to mind regardless of the time that has passed. I think I will never be free from these thoughts because one way or another they form part of my life.

From this terrible circumstance that Mary had to live through, I now, more than ever, feel beautiful and profound feeling of affection to see a boy or girl, but also great contempt for those who mistreat and abuse them. Children come into the world to bring joy to their parents. It's like a blessing that comes from heaven. It's a great joy!

Before arriving in the United States, I worked for more than eighteen years in a bank that fostered growth nationwide until 1991; and yet, I felt obligated to take leave without pay due to Mary's illness. My life changed, I was no longer the executive with many perks and benefits. I became a "cab driver" in order to survive and put food on the table for my children. At that time, being a cab driver in Lima was looked down upon; now I don't know since I haven't lived in Peru for more than fifteen years. The lack of employment opportunities forced many people to make a living one way or another; you could see all types of professionals acting as cabdrivers.

My life became extremely difficult during my unemployment, working seven days a week in the car. Many times I had to work sick, with a fever, with infections, tired, listless, dull, and of course with all of the risk and danger that the type of job implied. Many times I was worried to see that the day was ending and I hadn't yet earned enough for the following day. I had to find money for food and for the monthly household expenses... It was unbearable! There was no room for excuses. I always reminded myself: "You are the father; you have to do everything possible so that your home can keep moving along". Of course I was overflowing with hardships, to me our money wasn't enough at all.

The car that I drove was very old and constantly breaking down, adding many expenses to our already impoverished and chaotic economic situation. Sometimes, in the middle of the night, I had to try to "fix" the car, either lying on the ground to secure the exhaust pipe or burning my hand to try to correct a problem with the engine. Because of the time I spent at this job I learned how to do repairs in some way in order to avoid having to pay a mechanic. Other times, I had to push the car with passengers inside so that the car would start. The money I made was not enough to fix it opportunely.

I remember one day while working, I hit a very fancy and expensive car. The owner, in this unfortunate situation I was experiencing, decided to let me go to avoid, he said, passing him any of my bad luck. Of course I "flew" out of there before the distinguished and wealthy gentleman changed his mind.

I had to wait longer than necessary to change the engine oil or the worn tires that were always in bad shape. I remember I would buy used, cheap tires that would at least last a little while and that way I would avoid spending money on new tires. I was also constantly evading from the traffic police to avoid fines for the obvious car damages or for the lack of annual inspections and traffic controls needed to operate a vehicle.

It was five years of a terrifying and miserable life, one that I didn't see an escape from. I had fallen to the lowest place, full of despair, complexes, bitterness and fear of an uncertain future. I was terrified of becoming one of those indigents begging for money on the corner. Even now, when I see those people, I feel uneasiness within me remembering those difficult moments. One day, tired from the anguish of being caught in a "dead end" without an option in sight for a better future for my children or me, I made the decision to emigrate. I had to leave Peru and make every effort to find a better life…, a dignified and honorable life. I had to find the strength from wherever to emerge from that abyss. What a hard and traumatic decision! I had to separate myself from my children; I had to fight alone. The last straw was when, after so much effort, I was about to obtain a job as supervisor at a major pharmaceutical company in Lima. In the last stage of the hiring process, they saw I was over 40 years old and cancelled my offer. They didn't care about my extensive experience or my great desire to find the opportunity to demonstrate my ability to work…, that is why I finally made the decision to leave Peru.

Now you'll be able to see my intentions for writing this book. I have lived through all of this; in fact, I continue to live it every moment of my life. This is a true testimony of life, death and sickness, which I put at your disposal so that you can understand that you must always fight and not let yourself be defeated by adversity… "NEVER GIVE UP!" Value what you have! Strive to overcome the obstacles that afflict you, darken and spoil your life and consequently your future and that of your family that suffers watching you suffer.

## CHAPTER II
## MY FIFTEEN YEARS LIVING WITH
## CANCER…

With the help of a good Peruvian friend, I got my first job at a Mexican restaurant in Coconut Grove, a beautiful place considered a business district for the abundant commercial activity that it represented. I stayed there for almost seven years, working for over three years washing dishes, cleaning, helping servers and filling other positions. After that time and after arduous labor, the owners of the business decided to have faith in me and make me the office manager, which was a really huge encouragement and incentive for me during the times I was struggling to build a new life.

However, about a year after my arrival to this country my ordeal with cancer began, and with that, the sad and painful second part of my story. That happened almost fifteen years ago when one day, while I was working in the restaurant, I picked up something heavy and felt a rip inside of my body near my ribs on the right side. I kept working and wrapped a bandage around my waist trying to solve the problem in some way. I couldn't waste time. My kids waited in Lima for their maintenance and for the ability to continue with their lives thanks to the financial support from their father abroad. This is the case for many parents, who like I, look to economically support their families from outside of their own country.

After a while, one night while washing dishes, I felt a great, deep pain in the lower part of the right side of my back as if a knife had pieced my lung. At the hospital, after many long hours in the waiting room, a doctor saw me and said it was nothing, maybe because of my age my bones could be deforming causing the pain. She treated me very badly, with contempt, arrogance, and despotism, without showing any love for her profession.

By that time I had three jobs: at the Coconut Grove restaurant, cleaning houses and working nights at a tie factory where the owner would lock us in before leaving; the door was made of metal. The next day he would come to "free us". Our lives didn't matter to him only his business. I worked at folding the ties and cutting loose threads. I remember that I was assigned to work with an older Bolivian woman. I never imaged the speediness of this "old lady". She worked on the ties and passed them to me so I could do my part; it was piecework, the more ties that were made the more money we made. I was relieved when the lady took her break, but when she returned rested and full of energy, she worked me even harder…, and I finished off very tired.

I also had other "*cachuelos*" or little odd jobs that came up here and there. I had come here to work and that's what I was going to do. Among others, I remember when I went to fix a car that had a slight dent in the back. That was really terrible!... I left running when I finished the job. The car was worse than when I started. I didn't even wait to get paid.

After my visit to the hospital, within a few hours of arriving home, a call woke me up. It was the hospital. At that moment my life changed, it transformed forever. There was a spot in my lungs. Someone more responsible and careful noticed it. After several weeks of medical exams and an agonizing wait, everything turned into what I never expected to live through. I had cancer, non-Hodgkin's lymphoma. I was shocked, I cried, the anguish and despair appeared in my life again and in a very aggressive manner. My head was exploding; I felt I was going crazy.

I was alone, my children, the purpose of my life, were far away and waiting for me full of hope and expectation that they would be with me again and start a new life. I had asked them for patience and understanding, I had promised them that everything would be better and that soon we would be together again to live like a real, happy family, leaving behind the brutal suffering that we were subjected to in Lima. It was so hard for me to talk to them, hearing them talk to their father full of joy, confidence and assurance that everything would change. I made a great effort to hide my sadness and despair. While talking I worried that my voice would crack and I'd break into tears. I pretended to be happy and secure; I had to keep them from realizing what was happening to me. I didn't want to destroy their hopes and dreams of a better future, hopes and dreams that I had wrought into them when I made the decision to leave Peru.

My family of origin consisted of my dad "Cucho" and my mom Vilma, both from Lima and wonderful parents; Manuel "Pirucho", my older brother, Pedro "El Nono", the second one and Walter, the youngest. Sebastiana, our "Nana", accompanied the family.

My dad had always been a good example for us, he was a hard-working man, cheerful, a dancer, noble, calm, concerned and devoted entirely to his family, and to whom I was unable to give my final goodbyes because of living in this country "undocumented". I couldn't leave the country. One day while I was working, my brother Manuel, who arrived in this country after me, appeared out of nowhere, which he has never done before because of his other engagements, and he gave me the sad news. That was another big blow to my tired and troubled life full of hardships, misfortunes and sorrows. Again I felt the deep pain of losing a loved one, in this case my father, whom I always remember and miss, and still can't find the comfort or rid myself of the pain from his death, especially knowing that I will never be able to see him again. During his funeral, I spent the whole time calling Lima on the phone, trying to accompany him in some way. My father, like a good dad, knew that something was wrong by the tone of my voice when we talked. He was very understanding and did everything necessary to help his children. My dad worked all of his working life in a leading bank in Peru.

My mom, a schoolteacher, is a true example of struggle and honor. She is a disabled woman; but with much effort she earned her degree in Elementary Education at the respectable age of 39, while sick and after raising us. She always showed her desire for improvement; however, her health kept deteriorating more and more each day. Now she is 81 and retired.

Sebastiana Suyón, the "Nana", born in Piura, a beautiful city in northern Peru, has the well-deserved seat of honor as my second mother. She came into our home before I was born, when she was only 14 years old... and she stayed forever. She sacrificed her life for the love she had for us. With her care, affection and dedication she helped to shape us. Nana has lived with the family for sixty years and now, at 74 years old, she is still by my mother's side.

No one knew what I was going through... How sad! I had no one to share those moments with. I was completely alone. The great question was, after all that suffering in Lima, had I come to the United States to die?

Like any disease, and more so with it being the first time, it is very difficult to accept and understand it, especially when it dealt with "cancer". Fifteen years ago, this disease meant dying. Although, in truth, in spite of the advancements of science, each day we continue to see more and more people dying of cancer.

Can you imagine receiving this kind of news after all the other disasters? You feel the world cave in completely…, it crushes you. How do you run away? Where do you run? How can you turn back time? How do you jump over this new obstacle? Fear invaded my entire body and it kept eating away at my mind, every day, every hour and every minute of my life. I had no rest, no respite; it was permanent, persistent, and overwhelming.

Why me? The question of all time, as if the disease had a type of preference of some kind, it attacks children, teenagers, adults and the elderly, men and women of all social and economic statuses. It doesn't matter who you are, what your name is or where you come from. There you go, probably directly to your end.

All of this was added on to the fact that I spoke no English. How could I understand what the doctors and nurses were telling me? What were they doing to me? Where were they taking me? You feel lost and the looks confuse you. They are talking about you but you don't know about what. You feel strange, disturbed and helpless. You feel you've become a real life "guinea pig", a term that is referred to those animals that give their lives to science to help humanity find cures for diseases.

At the onset of the disease I was lucky enough to fall into the hands of a Mexican doctor, who became my friend. We spoke Spanish. He helped me get through that period of almost one year until I overcame the disease based on chemotherapy injected into a vein. I remember that the nurses came in wearing a special outfit and on one occasion I saw the red injection. Science has advanced and for the treatment of cancer, a "Port-A-Cath" also known as a "port" is used. It is a titanium device that is placed inside the chest and it allows catheters to be connected with the machines through needles.

When I finished with the first cancer, I underwent radiation treatments in the damaged area to burn the tumor or what was left of it. That is how I managed to expand the list of cancer "survivors". The doctor said that if the cancer did not return in four years, it would never return again.

Once again I started to live full of faith, hope and with the vision of further pursing my dreams, the reason why I came to this country. Almost three years of a normal life passed, and when I forgot about the terrible incident, unfortunately the cancer returned, and it returned so many times that I now find myself trying to save my life after the fifteenth time in fifteen years. The tumors appeared in different parts of my body: the neck, behind the tongue, groin, stomach, near the intestines, etc.

During all these years of relentless struggle, I had to go through numerous, devastating and terrible chemotherapy treatments, withstanding the awful side effects. They were so bad that many times I did not want to go back to the hospital for fear of having to feel those side effects.

The times I had to be admitted to the hospital were and continue to be very frustrating because of my restless nature. That fact causes me great sadness. Among other sad experiences, I remember that at night the nurses woke me up often to apply drops to my eyes to prevent drying and also to check on my vital signs. Other times the treatments were carried out through outpatient, as they are now. My doctor knows how difficult and traumatic it is for me to be hospitalized. I am still subjected to new and different experiments in search for a cure to my disease in order to save my life.

At the beginning of this illness and due to my chemotherapy treatments and its side effects, I felt obligated to leave other jobs and only continue working at the Mexican restaurant. I left house cleaning that had been so difficult to get, and only kept one, that of a lady named "Kary", an Argentinean-American woman who had a beautiful Mediterranean-style home, similar to the ones that existed in the ancient city of Pompeii, providence of Naples, Italy. This beautiful property, located in the city of Miami, has marble floors and corridors that go from one side of the house to the other. I got the job one day as I was waiting for the bus and a girl I met at that moment, after talking and getting to know my situation, decided to help, trust and recommend me. Mrs. "Kary" was very generous with the salary, but was very serious and demanding at work; she stood behind me to supervise my work, which made me nervous. She quickly realized that I did not know anything about cleaning houses, but she had the patience to teach me. With her I learned how to clean houses. I had never done it before. I come from a home where I was spoiled, where I didn't even have to make my bed. My mom and our "Nana" always pampered me before and after getting married. I was one spoiled child... What a change, right?

This woman had a big heart. Some times she picked me up from my "residence", a tiny little room in Miami, those that they call "studios" to appear more glamorous, full of cockroaches like all of the old houses in that city, but it was located on the beach..., at least that was a good start for living in Miami Beach. She would take me to the hospital to get my treatments and talked to the doctor about my health situation as if we were family or perhaps better than that. I also worked for this lady as coordinator for the parties she had in her home, such as "Thanksgiving day", a traditional and important day of celebration for the American community where each year, on the fourth Thursday of November, they participate in activities and dinners of thanksgiving. Other times I also worked as bartender, which I knew nothing about, but no one complained; instead, guests were very happy with my strange combinations in the drinks they asked for, names of drinks I had never heard in my life, worse yet if they ordered in English... I did the best I could to please the most exquisite tastes. I imagine that more than one person disagreed with my work, but the atmosphere was so happy, jovial and friendly, that there was no room for complaints... After all, it didn't matter; I was this woman's protégé. We had a great time, her especially, after a few "*vinitos*" or glasses of wine. I continue to talk to this special and unique lady, recalling the "old" times and her beloved husband, an American gentleman with wonderful and unique human qualities, whom unfortunately recently passed away.

# CHAPTER III
# CANCER RETURNS TO MY LIFE...

After a long process and many expenses, my two children were finally here by my side. I had reached my "big dream" of reuniting with them in the United States of America. Having my children was my greatest joy and happiness, a huge incentive to keep fighting for a better future. I felt truly happy.

We left the *"cuartucho"* where we were living and moved to an apartment facing the ocean in the city of Miami Beach. We bought new furniture. We were reaching the desired standard of living and what I had fought so hard for. I still remember the joy on my children's faces when they saw the truck arrive with our new furniture for our home.

We lived close to "Bal Harbour", the best shopping center in the city, located in an exclusive area of Miami. Everything was going great. I bought a new car. We traveled. In short, everything was great. I remember that we went to New York City for vacation. We were like "the perfect family", very happy, with problems just like any other normal family, but most importantly we were together... What more could I ask of life! I had managed to recover from and overcome the terrible problems I had lived through in the past.

Juan Carlos, the youngest of my children, arrived first. He suffered a lot at the beginning to adapt. He had to accompany me to work, he couldn't stay at home along because he was too young and because of the risks of dangers. I felt so sad watching him, a child, have to spend each day with me just waiting for the school year to start. My heart broke seeing him cry inconsolably. I only wanted the best for him. Juan Carlos missed his mom, his family and friends very much. Finally the day arrived when Juan Carlos would start his life as a student. I was sure that everything would be different and better for him. Unfortunately it wasn't like that. It was truly a very hard time for him, but much harder for me, trying to be father and mother to a child who was not happy living his new life. At that time, Peru had no future for young people. Many of them with a lot of luck went to the university but when they became professionals they had nowhere to work. It was a great opportunity for him to come to this country, it was just a matter of time before he would adapt. He was going to find friends and he would adapt much more easily. That was my greatest hope and I was willing to do whatever was necessary to make that happen and in that way, reach the goal of seeing him happy.

Once the school year ended, Juan Carlos returned to Lima for vacation. It was very hard to convince him to return to the United States of America; he did not want to come back. After long conversations we arrived at an agreement. To not make the story long, Juan Carlos is now 25 years old, lives in Miami, has a good job, speaks English, and goes to Lima as many times as he wants. He is very happy living in this country. Of course that doesn't mean that he nor Foncho nor I have given up our Latin roots. We are very proud of where we came from, and we share all of this with pleasure and delight our good, kind and friendly American friends.

Foncho, my oldest son, arrived six months later, after an intense and tedious process and because of the excellent guidance from a great Columbian friend, whom I will be grateful for all my life for his generous help. Foncho did adapt easily because he came as a 16 year old and he wanted the opportunity for a better future. He enrolled in an excellent, well-known community college to learn English. He always put in great effort and was hard-working, and now has a supervisory position at a global corporation.

When everything was all settled, when I was full of enthusiasm and expectation for the future, when joy and peace reigned in my home, when my children were on the right path, when all of the greatest efforts and sacrifices made sense..., my health again began to break down. Never did I imagine that the cancer would return to ruin my life once again, this time it was located on the back of my neck. Again I was subjected to intense medical exams, to the fear and worry.

Now, after all of these long years of struggle, I have four "mouths" in my chest, three of which represent many years of using catheters, these tubes that were placed in my chest, which bothered me and caused difficulty sleeping. A few times these catheters were removed from my chest when it appeared that I was healed. On the fourth "mouth", on the left side of my chest, I have had a "Port-A-Cath" for many years that I hope to have removed one day once I regain my health.

This time different doctors care for me, and once again the powerful chemotherapy treatments and their horrible and unbearable side effects put a dent in me. It's truly torturous. Every time that the cancer returns it takes over almost one year of my life.

After beating one of my episodes of cancer, a bone marrow transplant that my doctor recommended took place, hoping that the cancer would no longer return to my body. I put my life on the line. During twenty-one days I was isolated, immersed in chemotherapy to destroy the bone marrow in my body. I was kept alive with only the very necessary cells. Then, they transplanted the "new" bone marrow, which was really the same bone marrow after being cleaned and treated with chemicals. I accepted this with the hope and assurance that the cancer would no longer show up and that I would be able to live free of this scourge from society.

I remember that one of those nights, in the hospital for the bone transplant, I felt a reminder from God to not be tense and not fight against the chemotherapy. The idea was to let this "poison" do its job inside my body. That's when I realized that relaxing my shoulders was a great relief, it liberated my nervous tension and I was able to rest. Since then I always use this method of relaxation.

After that terrible event I could not be in contact with people to avoid any infection that could be fatal; therefore, I couldn't return to work. We didn't even have enough to eat. Foncho had to leave school to work and help out during those difficult moments. I went to my job begging for them to let me work, but they asked that I be completely recovered before returning. Unfortunately, I looked awful, I was extremely thin, didn't have hair, evidently I appeared very sick. I needed to work regardless of the state of my health, but I couldn't do anything to fix this situation.

Once recovered, we agreed to move to North Carolina, taking advantage of an offer I received, and also wanting to learn to speak English better. I loved the idea of being able to speak English well; in fact, in the near future I would love to be able to speak French, which would give me the opportunity to be able to communicate with most people in the world. It was very difficult for me to learn and practice English living in Miami, my American friends liked to speak Spanish in that city. I tried to speak it, I tried hard, but every time I greeted them in "English" they would respond in Spanish..., I was never going to learn the language in that way.

At first we struggled to adapt, but finally we succeeded. It was a new dawn, a new beginning..., a new life. It was like renewing and continuing to build the path to my fulfillment and that of my children.

Unfortunately, when everything was going as well as expected, when I felt strong, with high expectations for the future, working and studying, with an enormous desire to succeed and finally achieve all of my dreams... the cancer once again returned. I looked for the doctor who had recommended the bone marrow transplant, trying to find an explanation. All of that sacrifice that transplant cost was in vain, without counting the illusion I had of being a healthy man building a better life with my children. When I found the doctor, he told me that my body didn't respond to the transplant and he expressed his opinion that I maybe should do it again.

On another note, in my struggle to cure this disease, I acquired enormous medical debt that filled my life with anguish. Thank God I have always fought looking to find a way to pay these debts. The best thing to do is to step up and confront economic problems; it's tedious and very difficult, but not impossible. Hospitals have to find a way to recover their expenses spent on your recovery. I recognized that if you acquire a debt, the correct and decent thing to do is to make major effort to repay it, but I find it impossible to make payments on separate accounts, which, in my opinion, is absurd from every point of view. That happened to me in Miami and here in North Carolina. How can you pay each one of the accounts when there are so many? I suggested consolidating the bills into one and making gradual and fair monthly payments. I struggled greatly to be understood until finally I succeeded and I was able to avoid ruining my good credit. Thank God I am now lucky enough to have excellent health insurance through the company in which I work.

Upon leaving Florida, I had managed to negotiate all of my health debts. It's fair to say it was very difficult to accomplish this "great goal". I walked around every hospital office in Miami seeking an agreement, many doors were closed but I managed to open others. I am proud to say that, despite of my great economic problems that branched from this disease, my credit in the United States of America is very good. Why?... Because that's what I wanted!

Recognize all of your doubts, never you're your back on them, face your responsibility and find the most convenient solution. Fight to settle them, to be heard, to be understood, and that way you will avoid ruing your credit, which is so important in this country.

Once more I tell you…: You can achieve what you want with your dedication, astuteness, tenacity, hard work and effort! Don't give up with the first obstacle, fight to overcome all of your problems. The most important thing is to achieve your goals. You can't imagine how good you will feel when you are successful based on your personal effort. It doesn't matter if you have to try once or many times, trust me that you will always finish winning.

## CHAPTER IV
## LEARNING TO FIGHT AGAINST THE
## EFFECTS OF THE TREATMENTS...
## AND MY INTERNAL ANGUISH...

Cancer is a disease that comes with one purpose...: to end your life. It makes you suffer, demoralizes you, depresses you, destroys you, it gets inside your body and your mind. It slowly annihilates you. You feel like it's eating you alive, both physically and psychologically, and as if that's not enough, it "marks" you by balding you as a result of the medical treatments, which has a huge social impact. It's like a punishment, and the influence is even more damaging and disturbing in women. Ladies love their hair and they feel hit in the depth of their pride.

How do you feel? The usual question. You don't even know the answer. Bitter, lost, frustrated, with your mind outside of your body; or like in my case, two people inside of me, one sick and the other one struggling to overcome the trauma of the cancer and its effects. Your body does not respond to your energy. Your mood is low to the ground. You feel uncomfortable, everything bothers you, you can't even stand yourself. Your mind runs at one-hundred miles per hour and your body at ten. You feel just as much physical pain as you do moral pain to see yourself like that. You ask yourself so many questions, you don't have an answer to them. The side effects of all of these treatments are extremely difficult and scary. I remember that one day I went to eat at a Mexican restaurant located near my house, trying to overcome those effects. The owner, my friend, watching me suffer filled her eyes with tears.

The "chemo" enters your body to kill the cancerous tumors, but what other organs will it damage on its way?... Who knows.

How do you control what seems impossible to control?... How do you get taken over by the effects of the chemotherapy?... How can you face and overcome them?... Who can help you?

No one, no one else but YOU…, ONLY YOU. Everything, absolutely everything depends on you!

I know how difficult it is to face and control all these feelings that arise. There isn't medicine that makes you better. I have tried looking for help with my problem by taking different types of medications, which have been constantly changed without any positive results. Finally, and after much suffering and a lot of thinking, I was able to find a marvelous and extraordinary medicine…: "YOUR OWN STRENGTH AND WILLPOWER". Maybe it sounds like insignificant words, but it's the truth, it's the only way to fight for yourself, and with that strength you can also help others. It's the best way. You can't imagine how marvelous it is to discover, know, make use of and develop this powerful, exuberant, extraordinary, valuable, magnificent and overwhelming strength that lives inside of you.

If this were said by another person who has not gone through or is not going through this, I would not believe it for any reason. Anyone can say what they want or create fictional situations to take advantage of, but only those who live through these terrible and adverse circumstances like I have can express what one really feels on the inside. I am going through all of this at this moment while I am still trying to save my life.

Everyone asks themselves...: What can I do to escape this prison? Many say that it's not that easy or simple. The struggle is daily and in every moment of your confused and startled life. There is no rest. It seems never ending. My sincere and brotherly advice is that you don't give up for any reason. I know that what you feel inside is terrible and very difficult to describe. I don't know how many times I have felt a great frustration and impotence turn into a terrible and salvage moral pain...: the "soul pain" which I referred to earlier. Just as I explained at the beginning of this book, the first time I discovered this pain was watching my daughter fight for her life as a little 5 year old. For that reason, and for many more, she is and will continue to be my "great inspiration". I don't have words to describe, salute and admire her bravery at her young age. That is why I wish to emphasize the great example she left us of courage and bravery. Now we have a representative in heaven, our Mary, our "heavenly angel".

Many sick people remain in their bed because according to them they don't have strength to get up or to do anything; they even neglect their personal hygiene. Their house becomes their "fortress", although I would better say their "cemetery". They don't know the damage that they're doing to themselves by not putting in the effort to change that negative outline of their lives. That makes them even sicker. It's like living inside of a vicious cycle, an unhealthy and exhausting environment.

"I don't feel like doing anything", "I don't care what I look like", "no one is going to see me", "no one will notice if I smell good or bad". Cancer loves this type of "customer"; in reality it's its favorite kind. Your neglect doesn't help, it hurts you and later it minimizes you so that it kills all of your strength, enthusiasm and consequently your life. If that is what you want, "I congratulate you because you're on the right track toward the end". I know it's not easy to cope with this situation; I have been living it for the past fifteen years.

The same day of my treatments I went directly to my office to continue working. How "crazy"! How "brute"! How can Carlos do that?... That, dear reader, is the most fervent proof of my desire to fight for life. God helps me and I put in the effort and push myself until I can't push any further to comply with that divine support.

Upon leaving the hospital, many times I have felt as though I was burning alive and other times as though my face and hands were full of tiny needles. You become extremely sensitive.

I go to the hospital in my car every time. I don't want anyone to take me. I like to go on my own. I thank my children and my friends for their concerned to take me to the hospital, but that makes me feel bad, like a disabled person.

After the winter treatments, and dealing with the cold weather in North Carolina, my face becomes very sensitive and shrinks, my eyes narrow and I feel the pressure from the treatments. After many years I got used to living with this discomfort. Moreover, my pinky fingers have deformed due to the treatments and cause me pain. I am someone who enjoys giving a handshake to my good friends, without thinking about the pain that it's causing me, that I almost don't even feel it because I don't want to feel it. My "WILLPOWER" is made of iron and my "ENTHUSIASM" and "WILL TO LIVE" are even stronger. Many of you, my family and friends know me and would not let me lie.

My VANITY is my great companion, I would say my best friend. It helps me greatly. I don't like to look bad. I make an effort so that I look good, regardless of how bad I may feel. I don't accept or let myself decline.

I lose weight with each treatment. I can't sleep well, I don't even need it. Sometimes I sleep a few hours and other times just here and there. My nerves are severely agitated, but I'm still smiling and loving this beautiful life with an unbridled and an acute passion. This is what I want to pass on to you. You can do the same if you so wish and if not, what are you complaining about? After all, your luck is what you yourself create. Don't expect people to watch, admire, and praise you for the effort you make. That is for you and for your own wellbeing. Don't live from others or for others. It is your life that's at stake. Do it for yourself and for your family that at the end is the one that mostly suffers. Your family needs you, loves you and wishes to see you doing well. You are in a seat of honor for them. Lean on, protect yourself in and rely on the unconditional love that they profess to you. Use the precious energy you have, radiate great positivism and, consequently, you will receive the same. Fight for "THE MIRACLE OF YOUR LIFE". Don't let your precious dreams, desires and illusions be destroyed…, fight to live a dignified life full of health, passion, energy and love. Invest your time in becoming a good example for others. Lend a hand to those who are weaker because on the road to your development and improvement you were one of them. Put a lot of passion into everything you do, your ideas, goals, short term and long term projects, and pursue them until you achieve them. Look to reach your goals and later enjoy the outcome of your efforts. The victory is yours. For this reason, and much more, "PASSION FOR LIFE… A message to the willpower" is the name I chose for my book. Because of the way I am, it didn't cost me a lot of effort to come up with the title of the book.

In everything I write I hope I am not changing or infringing on any universal rule. Nor do I wish under and any reason or circumstance to impose my personal opinions. My intention in my revealing here is a profound and great desire to help everyone who in one way or another suffers and desires to emerge victorious from his or her problems. I don't pretend to be a "Superman" because I'm obviously not. I am a common, ordinary person, full of great humility and simplicity. What I want through this book is to convey my strength, energy and rebelliousness to help in some way find relief from the illnesses and the "limitations", to which I declare, openly and forcefully, that "THEY DON'T EXIST". You are capable of building the good and destroying the bad. Your mind is infinite and immeasurably powerful.

This entire compendium of experiences lived by me I offer to you in this book. Don't you think it's ideal to have "power tools" to guide you in life? Hopefully you'll be able to take advantage of them in the best way. I do it for you, hoping that it will inspire you, motivate you, and lead you to be better every day.

Awaken all of your gifts. To name a few: intelligence, knowledge, wisdom, love, etc. Also, your values: perseverance, willpower, respect, integrity, dignity, spirit of service, endurance, kindness, happiness, courage, friendship, generosity, gratitude, equity, etc. It is for your wellbeing. Conduct an introspection and see how much "virgin" wealth is within you, wealth waiting to explode for your own benefit and that of those who surround you. That source of wealth is so powerful that it will broaden you. What joy you will feel when you free yourself from your problems based on your own resources. Break the chains that have had you bound and frustrated for so long. Break your relationship with your prefabricated situations and prejudices that only cause harm. Avoid believing and following limiting situations typical of the beliefs of some cultures. Reject that relationship, fight and strive to change and to leave behind what you don't need and harms you. From now on "I CONGRATULATE

YOU" for accomplishing this important and momentous change in your life.

There are days when I feel my body losing balance, I feel pain, the muscles in my legs turn to knots and I feel that I'm carrying bricks as I walk, and that's not counting the fact that I can't sleep well. I have to push myself and find the strength to overcome this situation before it finishes me.

In May of 2011 I went to the hospital for an evaluation exam after twelve rounds of chemotherapy, one a week. The results were a big surprise...: the tumor was the same. The doctor couldn't help showing his concern. The rounds of that new treatment were suspended because there was no reason to continue "torturing" me at that time. The only thing left was to wait for another possible option to save my life.

That afternoon, after the unpleasant, depressing and sad results, I realized that I had to react, with that negative and defeatist attitude I wasn't going to accomplish anything, on the contrary, I would have been giving up and helping the disease finish me off. I wasn't going to accept this situation. I have a family that I love with all of my heart and I wish to continue by the side of those who comprise it, supporting them and watching them reach their goals. I also still have my own goals and a great desire to live and succeed in my life as a professional. I always say that I didn't come to the United States to die but to succeed.

All of this, my immense faith in the mercy of the Creator, my faith in myself and the prayers and concern of all my family and friends around the world are what have kept me alive until now. I have to keep fighting with much spirit and get enthusiasm from wherever I can. I love life and I wish to continue living. Therefore, I created and imposed my own rules:

<u>FIRST</u>, my immense faith in God leads me to place my life in His powerful and compassionate hands.

SECOND, maintain a good appearance and attitude above all.

THIRD, do not stop smiling under any circumstance.

FOURTH, keep my pride very high.

FIFTH, strengthen my enthusiasm to its highest level of expression.

SIXTH, maximize the level of my willpower.

SEVENTH, do not let thoughts of death, doubt and fear invade my mind.

EIGHTH, make the feelings of sadness and discouragement disappear from my mind.

NINTH, elicit and obtain all that brings me joy and makes me laugh.

TENTH, be more eager in my desire to succeed and "eat up" the whole world.

ELEVENTH, put the disease behind me and not let it conduct or ruin my life.

TWELFTH, celebrate and be thankful each day for the fact that I'm still alive.

I know that after all of that feeling of power and triumph, a great void might invade, accompanied by the doubt and immense fear to "challenge" the unknown. I know this feeling perfectly.

The questions are many. What am I about to face? How will I overcome all of this? How can I be sure that the results will be in my favor and that I will come out ahead? Where am I going to get the strength to accomplish that? Will I be able to overcome it or am I walking directly toward my demise? You feel something terrible inside of yourself. Your mind works strongly, very intensely, looking and looking for a way out, an answer. You feel horrible, completely out of place, terrified. It's a cold inner feeling that makes you restless and torments you to the max. You feel that you're going crazy. You feel that the world is most hostile and harsh with you. That strange and strong internal feeling is what I call "depression".

Depression is cancer's best friend. You cannot imagine the way in which it destroys you. It creates a ghost of terror inside of you. It submerges you in great anxiety. It strongly damages you. It eats you alive little by little. You feel something inside of you that causes despair with no control. Do not let that enter your life. Flatly reject that negative feeling... TELL IT NO! Change the frequency of your mind. Think of all of the beautiful things life has to offer. Force yourself to have a smile on in all of your actions. When I feel its presence, I immediately leave for a change of scenery. I meet up with old friends or look to make new ones anywhere; I'll even get a drink, although I should clarify that I'm not a drinker, I never have been nor will I be. When I am with my friends or outside of my home I never speak about my health problem. On the contrary, I joke, I laugh until I can't anymore, and that way I have a good time. You can't imagine how beneficial it is to change that frequency. I drive home with the radio at a decent volume, singing, drumming on the steering wheel trying to follow the beat of the music, as happy as can be.

Many times, after the treatments, with the desire to fight to get ahead, I have to put in a huge effort to force my body to get out of bed, I feel as though I can't, but I hear a voice inside that drives me to not let myself sink into that state of discouragement. My body resists that effort, but my desire to live is truly powerful and influential. Then, upon showering I have felt my body shake, weak and damaged by the contact with the water. That is one of the tests that I am able to surpass as I fight for my life and not let myself get beat by the disease and the maddening side effects of the treatments. That effort is extremely effective for me. Copy it and imitate it, it will help you; it's for your own good…, it's for your life.

One day, already tired from not being able to sleep and knowing that my nerves were extremely disturbed, I made a decision, a "big decision"…: I filled myself with a lot of courage and determination and I decided to no longer take my pills for sleeping or for my nerves. Another reason I made this decision came when I was in Miami for a few days visiting my son Juan Carlos and I forgot to bring my pills for sleeping and my nerves. I couldn't sleep because I depended on those medicines. That was frustrating for me, I felt ashamed of myself for being cornered and subjected to live with these kinds of "conditions". Also, due to the chaotic state of my weakened nerves, I took a pill aimed for people who had a risk of suicide. It got that far. However, I made the decision to not continue my life tied to these chemicals. I didn't want to depend on pills to make my life "falsely normal", especially knowing and recognizing that I was capable enough to make that effort. At the beginning, it was incredibly hard to get on the right path. What a difficult fight! It seemed impossible. My body trembled. At times I felt the desperate sensation of having to go back to the pills. I thought I couldn't do it and that was extremely difficult for me but I fought and I fought the best that I could. After a long and tough battle, I was able to achieve it. Of course in order to reach this level of development I went through long periods of getting to know my body and my powerful internal strength. Now you can try to jump over obstacles and to achieve your overcoming with this irrefutable testimony of survival. If you are aware of what you have, then YOU CAN find the solution for yourself. Here I am just sharing my personal experience, and I know that not everyone is the same, that's why you should always consider and listen to the advice from your medical professional.

Sometimes I hear people who have problems say, "I don't know what I have", "I don't know what's wrong". That is a BIG LIE! You do know what you have but you deny it because you fear feeling like a frightened, weak, and dejected person. You prefer to choose to fill yourself with pills, many times unnecessarily, to support your weakness and to calm your nerves. You lie to yourself. We have to start recognizing our problems with humility, sincerity, integrity, and above all with commitment, determination and nobility in order to solve them. Once more, for that you have your marvelous and powerful "MENTAL STRENGTH".

The inability to sleep is really disastrous and breaks the stability of your nerves. I was thinking about what I could do to overcome this problem and I came to the conclusion and resolution to not fight against it. Most people who do not sleep feel disturbed, desperate, out of control, and grumpy. Imagine in my case, after the dreadful chemotherapy treatments, not being able to sleep, and going into work the following day, trying to give it all I've got. One has a responsibility to fulfill and should do it, that's what one is paid for. One can't take advantage of those who so generously worry about providing help and support.

In my sleepless nights I put my mind to work. I think of my projects to be more successful. I also think about other options to develop and improve my work.

Even though I cannot sleep, I fulfill my obligations, always wearing a big smile because others aren't to blame for one's problems and deserve consideration and respect. I am very pleased to work for Members Credit Union, a non-profit financial institution that helps low-income individuals achieve their financial goals. The gentile officials of this noble institution, headed by the President, Jack Braswell Jr., have been very sympathetic to my health problem. I work hard to honorably and completely fulfill my commitment of devotion and dedication to my job and in return I respond well to such understanding and generosity. I try my best to look good and not give the impression of being a sick person, and believe me I am somehow managing.

I don't deny what I feel. My body is without energy, my eyes are dry, my legs are weak and heavy at the same time, I feel a hard weight on my head, I am dizzy, my body aches, every time I get up out of my desk chair I have to make a great effort to walk. I would like to sleep during the day since I cannot at night. I live with "needles" on hands, my body is full of welts that itch all the time, which I try to alleviate very carefully to prevent breaking the skin and to not acquire an infection. I recognize that I am a very sick person, but with a profound determination and resolution of finishing with this illness as soon as possible and returning to being a normal person like everyone else. WHY NOT?!

All of this strength was not created just for me, nor is it for my exclusive use. You also have it and its use or waste is only up to you. Use your powers; do not deny such a wonderful "benefit" that God has given you.

I continue doing my work with much dedication, optimism, loyalty, care, devotion and enthusiasm. I am always trying to be very efficient and productive, and to look for ways to enhance and optimize my work as much as possible. I take pride in knowing I fulfill my responsibilities fully, for which I count on a well-deserved reputation and prestige.

Because of how busy I always am, I somehow forget about my health problem. I love the idea of being useful, helpful, cordial, friendly, understanding, and amiable. I see people daily, I talk to them both in and out of the office trying to help as much as possible. My work doesn't have a schedule for me, and yet on the weekends I do my best to promote my institution. Also, I decided to return to my work activities outside of the office, attending business meetings, trying to promote and develop our social and financial objectives in the community, both Latino and U.S. American.

Currently, and after much effort, I am the respected and recognized Vice President of Latino Services of Members Credit Union. I have the support of a large group of people, Latino members who trust my work. I have many Latino and U.S. American friends who support me at all times and in an incredible way. There is no reason I would ever disappoint the trust they have in me. I have created something big based on great effort.

At the beginning, when I arrived at this institution, I was the only Latino, I didn't speak English well and it was very difficult to establish myself in my position for lack of communication with other areas. Nevertheless, they trusted in me. I fought in a bold way to move ahead with my work. I invented my own resources to develop my work. People enjoyed being a member of the unofficial "Friends of Carlos Club". How could I let this wonderful effort go to waste due to my illness? My goals are to continue fighting for everything that has been done and to try to do more and be better every day responding to such appreciation, affection and understanding of my superiors.

Now, after eight years of hard work, I can assure you that we have become one of the financial institutions with the best personalized service in the state. In April 2011 I received recognition as the "Latino Leader of 2011", a

Hanesbrands, Inc. award, for my work with the Latino community in Winston-Salem in Forsyth County. This occurred during the "Spanish Nite" ceremony organized by the Hispanic League, an institution that works hard to help Hispanic youth realize their dream of pursing higher education.

I am constantly on local radio stations doing interviews and talking about the benefits of our company and the excellent personalized services that my noble institution offers the community. I also appear on various Latino newspapers with widespread circulation throughout North Carolina.

To my major satisfaction, I appeared on the front page of a major U.S. newspaper when I turned into reality my project of opening up my "Museo Latino" in my own office, and I consider it to be the first museum of its kind in America. This is one of my biggest and most ambitious projects, which I am very proud of. There came a day when I wished to do something different that would make my job more successful. I am someone who suffers from "job dissatisfaction" and I am always looking to do more things, but distinct things that will promote our good name. I love to innovate and create new things. Thanks to the appreciation and love of the members and friends of this great institution, I have come to collect many souvenirs from all of the Latino countries, which have filled my office. Through this museum I show the whole world the beauty and richness of our noble, beautiful and ancient Latin Heritage.

I also teach financial education conferences for youth of different educational centers, and I support other institutions in their important financial education programs for adults. I firmly and strongly believe that education is the key to the development of individuals and nations worldwide. I take the time to discuss perseverance in fighting for what one believes, and selfless support to others, among other issues of great importance. I also speak on the negative impact on society from the presence of gangs, drugs and everything that affects the normal development of a life. I also speak about my experience with cancer. With my life testimony I try to influence those young people to be convinced that one should always fight against any adversity and for a worthy and glorious future. Unfortunately, in all of my meetings I find someone who has a member of their family or a close friend dying of cancer.

I'm passionate about my job, my work is very nice, and I put in all my effort, love, and experience and enjoy it immensely. My goal is to help everyone who comes to see me, which I do with love and complete dedication. I can humbly assure anyone that the Latino community gratefully appreciates my work. My major concern is to always keep a very high PRESTIGE AND REPUTATION.

In my struggle to survive I use some self-help methods. For example, when I see the sun come out, I go to my patio to catch some of those solar rays, which in my opinion are extremely beneficial for me. That and a good suntan lotion give me a nice color to my skin and consequently a better personal presence. It makes me feel really good, gives me a radiant personality and in turn lifts my spirits, my desire to live and enjoy life. I love it! This personal therapy feeds my vanity. Don't you think looking good helps? It is a strong and powerful "tool" that I always use. It helps put my problems behind me. It is very effective; it changes one's suffering personality into a fervent desire to live. One feels energetic... and, best of all, it is available completely "free". All of this helps one understand that in the face of a great problem there is always a great solution.

As you are seeing in this story, I am humbly giving the elements that still keep me alive and with much hope that perhaps soon I can find a solution to my health problem. Meanwhile I try to help myself in some way. It has been fifteen years fighting for my life. Of course, at first I didn't know what to do. I was unfortunately immersed in a totally unknown world, alone, scared and helpless. I didn't have enough knowledge or experience necessary to "play" with other forms of aid.

Another important element for me is water. I drink it in abundance. It helps to clean the toxins out of my body and hydrates my organism. I eagerly drink water all the time and as much as I can.

At the beginning of my illness, something unusual happened to me. Due to my treatments, water tasted bad and had an unpleasant smell. We all know that water doesn't have a flavor or smell. Thankfully, this situation passed and now I enjoy this great gift from nature. I am completely confident that one day people will better recognize its richness.

When I started with this problem I had no one to give me any advice or encouragement to my hopeless life based on any real experience. I have never seen a life story like mine, and that is the reason that I share it in this book with the sole purpose of helping others. I give it to you and dedicate it as a message to your will power, to the greatness of your spirit, to your courage, strength, wisdom, enthusiasm and tenacity. BE BRAVE AND DECIDE NOT TO BE DEFEATED!

Medical science may at some moment give up hope for my health, but nobody is going to destroy or give up hope for my strength, my love and the passion I feel for life and my great desire to be a socially and morally successful person with an immense desire to love and be loved... I am aiming toward that find and will do everything possible to achieve it. MY PASSION FOR LIFE and my desire to succeed are clear, strong and powerful. I think I still have much to do in this world before reaching the side of the Almighty. I am sure of that, what's more, I feel that HE is with me, cares for me and gives me strength to continue with this fight. I also have members of my family in heaven who intercede for me...: my daughter, my dad, my brother Pedro who died of pancreatic cancer, Grandma Joan, my aunts

Dora, Olga and Victoria, among other loved ones. These are people who are now enjoying eternal life and who always demonstrated their love and understanding and whom I keep at the bottom of my heart.

Life, despite all the difficulties and hardships, is still beautiful to me. Look to do something more in your life, assume the responsibility to help others for the joy of doing it and make that an important, necessary and transcendental commitment. Put a lot of enthusiasm into everything you do, no matter how you feel and don't forget to add a smile to it all. Smiling feeds your spirit. Fight with adversity not against it, confront it, and try to get the positive out of its presence in your life. Keep fighting and earn "your place in life". Create your own energy, product of your own strength and try to understand what is happening to you. Do not find someone to blame because you won't find anyone. Maybe you're the only one because of your carelessness and lack of courage and determination that has permitted your problems to lead you directly to your disease. Work to fully exploit the magic of your marvelous mind to find your own solutions. Do not waste time waiting for others to do it for you. Look for the exit and trust me, you will find it.

In August 2011, after receiving the sad news that the tumor that lives near my intestines was still alive despite more than seven years of continuous treatment without rest in North Carolina, and seeing that the chemotherapy no longer worked in my body due to all of the years of receiving it, I was sent to the radiation area of the hospital. The doctors in that area, knowing that I had already been radiated in that part of my body, the right side of my stomach, considered it fatal to radiate again. Later they thought about radiating me through a vein or operating to take out the tumor and radiating that area afterward. None of those options met the expectations of the doctors because of how dangerous it was to my worn body. Finally, they sent me back to oncology. My experienced oncologist, a prestigious doctor and a recognized professional, very humane and a true friend, showed his concern for my health problem. This physician and his team of doctors and cordial and diligent nurses regained control of my illness. This is how I began my ninth try to save my life, this time through a new experiment that has helped other people with cases similar to mine. There were going to be sixteen sessions. In that attempt and because of its effects and my weight loss, at the fourth session they gave me a two-week break to recover and so that we could restart the twelve sessions that were still needed. However, at the sixth session that new attempt was canceled because nothing was achieved with it.

A short while after I started a new treatment that consisted of receiving a large injection of radiation through my "port". That was a new option to achieve the dream of regaining my health. It was a new experiment that according to statistics had already shown its efficiency in many with similar cases to mine and maybe could somehow help me. There were going to be eighteen sessions… It was terrible, I almost died. I started to lose weight rapidly, about two pounds per day. Even forcing myself to eat well, I ended up losing almost ninety pounds. Regardless of the numerous blood transfusions I received, the treatment was eating me alive internally, finishing off with my red and white cells, platelets, potassium, etc. I felt I was dying. One day my son Foncho found me in bed with a high fever. He took me to the hospital where they detected a severe infection in my abdomen due to the treatment. I was already feeling very bad but I was trying to overcome the problem like I always do, although I was not expecting such an infection. Each treatment is different and therefore so are its side effects. I had to be hospitalized for more than three days to again save my life.

During one of those days, Foncho obtained a civil marriage, and I was permitted, upon my insistence, to attend the ceremony for a few hours before returning to continue with my recovery. It was very moving to see my son get married. Regardless of my state of health, I wouldn't miss that great event of his life for anything. I felt very proud, as a father, of the effort that I made to make him and his wife feel my fraternal support.

As a consequence of this unsuccessful attempt, that treatment was also canceled because of the danger.

I have desperately fought to regain my weight, trying to eat, ignoring my constant and continuous diarrhea. There comes a moment when one just can not stop eating, has to keep trying, there is no point in getting tired of trying, if it's not done, one dies. What a great struggle it was trying to recover my appearance. That had never happened to me, especially to such an extent. That time the treatment was out to kill me, not only because of the damage to my health, but also because it touched one of the most important aspects for me, one of my greatest resources, my secret weapon…: "MY VANITY". I looked very bad.

It was incredible the extreme it reached. After showering it felt much sadness seeing my body all "skin and bones". I had to tighten my pants with rope so that they wouldn't fall. One day, a friend came to my office and surprised upon seeing me yelled... What happened to you?! I felt very bad, but I responded simply with a smile. I faced this unpleasant event with a profound feeling of "REBELLION AND REJECTION" to that unfortunate situation. I wasn't going be defeated and much less let myself be destroyed morally, which would have surely meant the sad end of me. I had been mortally hit in the deepest part of my being, but that rebellion and repudiation that I felt pushed me to emerge from that wretched situation and continue fighting. Again I had to rise from the rubble and fight to triumphantly arise from this new, terrible and disastrous event in my life.

In November I got to the hospital after the pertinent exams to know the state of my health. My hope was that since the treatment had done so much damage, it could, in some way, have an impact on the tumor. I was sure that the tumor had disappeared. That was my big hope. I was beginning to feel the sense of triumph and my desire to be on the path to arise. My chest was full of emotion imagining that it would finally be time for success in my desperate and long fight. I thought that life would finally compensate me for all of the years full of atrocious suffering…, it was only fair.

The countless times I've had to go to the hospital to receive news about my health, I have gone with the certainty that it's going to be a "great day" for me. Even now I still wish fervently that it would happen. My dream is to one day soon hear that beautiful phrase "cancer free".

But the news about my health shook and resonated within my body and blew my mind. I felt I would explode. Again I felt the disappointment and frustration. It seems as if life was laughing at me loudly and mocking my fervent desire to be healthy. I felt a punch to the face or the push that would finally make me fall. Unfortunately, the tumor was the same, nothing happened to it and, on top of everything, two new tumors had emerged in the stomach area. That totaled three cancerous tumors. There was no rest for me. Nothing helped me. I cling firmly and determinedly to life, but all indications are that life flat out rejects me.

Was the cancer pouring into my body? Was I going to die soon? It was imminent and necessary to start a new alternative. That is how I started the eleventh attempt to save myself from this ruthless evil. They were sixteen sessions, one every three months. My doctor told me that this new experiment was very successful and that it could help me. When I asked him what other steps we would take if it didn't work, he told me there were other options to keep me alive and that soon we would get good news to cure this disease.

My hope was based on that good news finding me in good time to save my life.

Once again, just like each time that I start a new treatment, I was informed and advised of the side effects of that new attempt, effects that I prefer not to pay attention to as to not affect my positivism.

At the end of each one of the sessions, and as usual with me, I go straight to my office to continue working trying to have a "normal" life. I have only missed work the times I have had to be admitted to the hospital.

Anyway, I am still full of faith and optimism, looking at life with high expectations and a great hope that each time we can find a cure. Accompanying this intrinsic desire is a smile on my face as evidence of great confidence that soon I'll be able to overcome this unfortunate and stormy situation. As far as I'm concerned I'm still here and will continue to be until God says so. I don't plan on giving up so easily. I won't do it. Thank you my God for giving me the strength not to give up and for my decision to defend my place in this life.

Before closing this chapter of my book, I want to say that everything expressed here is the result of my experience obtained through all of these disastrous years facing this disease. As I have stated, I do not desire or intend to change anything, nor do I desire this writing to be the last word on how to confront this problem nor do I encourage people to follow me fervently. All that I want is to help people find their own way out of their problems, outside of the conventional, regular and established way. I want to nourish you with a bright, bold, aggressive and arrogant spirit to defeat this and other terrible evils. Only God, whichever way you think of him, is the one privileged to make decisions about your life. I just want to express that YOU CAN help yourself using the powers that He has given to you as well as to all of his other children equally. Life is as difficult as you chose to make it. The path toward success is filled with failures and defeats. For example, I don't know how or when my beautiful and passionate life will end, but as far as I'm concerned, I am going to continue living the best way that I can, because I have the right to live a full, dignified and decent life, free from limitations and diseases. I will always keep looking at and facing all of my problems with a "defiant" smile. Remember that a great smile on the face doesn't mean an absence of problems; instead it means THE ABILITY to be happy above them. A good attitude is the key to success. I have my own goals very clear and I firmly believe that I am going to achieve them all. I have a lot of faith and trust, in the Almighty as well as myself.

To the reader, focus your life toward a main goal, to be a positive person, a good example of strive and perseverance…, a true winner, "five stars". Build don't destroy. The future of the world depends entirely on us, on our attitude, our effort and enthusiasm. We are completely responsible for our actions, the consequences of those actions and of our future. We are the same reflection of what we do. What you do always comes back to you. Radiate sympathy, trust and security. Own a great, bright personality. You're not lacking anything to do that, JUST MAKE THE DECISION TO CHANGE. Love and let yourself be loved. Break from the traditional and conservative. Create and innovate, seeking for the best for yourself and others. Open your window to the world, to the colors that wise nature gives for your immense joy and inspiration. You choose to live or die, laugh or cry, be strong or weak, your successes or your limitations, frustrations and misfortunes. Always be honest, compassionate, loyal, sincere and transparent. Reject hatred, fear, resentment and everything that limits you and makes you feel inadequate. Remember that being selfish make us miserable, that material things are not more important that feelings. Accept your challenges with integrity, boldness and courage. Never stop at anything… "BE FREE". Respect others and respect yourself. Be useful to society. Help out without expecting anything in return. Develop your powerful mind to the best of the best. Enlighten society and the world with A RADIANT AND BEAUTIFUL SMILE. And remember that the time on the clock never turns back.

LIVE INTENSELY AND FULLY ENJOY EVERY MOMENT OF YOUR LIFE!

# PART II

# LETTERS FROM MY FAMILY AND FRIENDS

*"Thank you to my family and to all my friends, who so kindly participated in my book by providing their input and opinions".*

*Carlos Patiño Effio*

## ADA PUERTAS
## PERU

Congratulations, Carlitos! You are such an inspiration. Your life has been a constant struggle. I have always admired your strength and integrity in the difficult times you have lived through, and finally through your fight against cancer. I am sure your book will be successful; I hope they will sell it in Lima. A big hug.

## ADDISON, MELANI AND
## ENRIQUE ROMERO
## MEXICO

Mr. Patiño, we thank God that we have you in our lives and for giving us the privilege to know you. Many times we doubted that angels exist, but we see one in you and are sure that you are not only for us but also for many more people. Thank you so much for having a heart so full of generosity and love. May God give you many blessings.

ADOLFO BRICEÑO
MEXICO

Dear Carlos, good luck with your book! Few of the people that I know and have known are able to face like you, with such joy and enthusiasm, the devastation of cancer. Your attitude is an example of integrity and bravery that should serve as a basic and essential manual on how to face adversity, in whatever form it may come.

AMÍLCAR ARROYO
PERU

Carlos Patiño means so much to me. I have known Carlos for thirty-eight years. I met him when we worked together in the Central

Mortgage Bank of Peru in Lima. His duties were directly related to the daily relations with the bank's employees and executives. I got to know him little by little, firstly as a co-worker and after as a friend. We spent time together during and after work. The similarity in age of our children meant we shared many life experiences.

I will never forget what a gentleman he was to everyone. He was always friendly, always smiling, offering a firm handshake and always trying to help others. He was always immaculately dressed, punctual, attentive, disciplined and fair in his decisions – a good friend.

After nearly twenty-six years, we met again here, in the United States – he lived in North Caroline and I in Pennsylvania.

From our conversations I learned that my wonderful friend was suffering from cancer and that he had endured many battles with it and was always triumphant, until now. I also learned that Carlos went through difficult times personally and professionally, having to work unimaginable jobs to support his family. He overcame those difficult moments little by little and found himself where is now. Carlos demonstrates how to be a human to the community. His role as Director of Latin Services in the financial institution in which he worked demonstrates his passion for service to others and his great strength to overcome obstacles.

The recognition that Carlos receives from the public now is just like the local opinion from Lima – he has remained the same man since I knew him in Lima. Carlos is a great human being that thinks of others before himself. With Carlos's smile he gives you his heart. He is the father that supports his children so he may later witness the joys of their triumphs. It is the executive, the Latin man who is a real example for others, as it was before. To describe Carlos Patiño in a few lines does not do him justice.

In closing, I hope you know the lessons you will learn in this book will give you the tools that many of us need when we feel lost and the labyrinth of life and believe that we are nothing. Through the pages of this book and from the history of his life, you will learn how to overcome pain, sickness, and loneliness like all limitations. You have in this book a guide and a reason to say, "Yes, Carlos was able to do it. Why not me?" You are triumphant, like Carlos. Like him, fight relentlessly to achieve your dreams and find the power that each of us has within ourselves. Never forget that God is our Creator, nor forget that the love of our parents, family and friends is the force that drives us to keep fighting.

Carlos, I admire you and I am so proud that you call me your friend, your "brother". Your lessons do not have borders… God bless you.

AMY SHELLBERG
UNITED STATES OF AMERICA

Carlos Patiño is the epitome of life. A very handsome Peruvian with a big heart, a great spirit and a passion for life that exceeds anything I have ever seen. I am privileged to call him a friend.

## ANA MARÍA ROJAS
## PERU

My dear Carlos, I don't have the words to tell you all that I feel. It has been more than thirty years that I have known you and you have always been a great friend to me. I have many memories of the time we worked together in Lima. You are a remarkable man for all you have achieved and for your fight against cancer. I am proud to have a friend like you, above all because you are a person of integrity, a wonderful father and an unconditional friend that has always been there when we needed a word of encouragement. I love and admire you. May God bless you, my great friend Carlos.

## ASHLEY PAIGE RELLA
## UNITED STATES OF AMERICA

I never knew how blessed I was that Carlos was to become part of my life. What I would learn from having him as a friend has enriched me. From day one, Carlos was always happy, smiling and full of life. Every day I am welcomed by a smile that hides an illness, and only recently I learned he was sick. How could that be? Never would I have suspected what this man was going through. His story is strong, compelling, it is a turn of beautiful emotions. He speaks openly and sincerely much like the way he chooses to live. I have never met a person who has desired and fought so hard to just simply live and love.

Carlos Patiño is not just a friend to me; he is a teacher, a reason to smile, a reason to live life! I will always take with me the simple lessons of a smile, the significance of "no time wasted" and "just be happy" when I need a push. He has given me lessons, that I now can pull out of my own pocket, open its pages, and use its words to put a smile on my face, when I too need to face the world. Simply put, he is the reason I am a better person today.

With all my heart and much respect.

## BECKY RIGGINS
## UNITED STATES OF AMERICA

Carlos you have been such an inspiration to me with your beautiful smile. When I felt bad I would see your face and know the pain you have been through and I no longer felt badly for myself. You mean so much to me. I look forward to many more years of your friendship and smile.

## CALIQUE MARTÍNEZ-HAGUE
## PERU

Well, Uncle, first of all I would like to commend you for your strength. You know that you have always been like a father to me just as Foncho, your son, has always been and will be like a brother. You have shown me so much and now, although I have not seen you for many years, you continue to teach me to have strength, faith and to fight against all adversity. You are a role model and your example is seen in your children.

From Lima, I send you a hug and a kiss on the cheek as I would a real father. Your nephew, as always, Calique.

## CARLOS ALFONSO PATIÑO
### CARLOS'S SON
### PERU

I am honored and proud to call Carlos Patiño "Dad". How to describe my father? A great fighter, a dreamer, positive, smiling, motivator and a role model. Ever since I can remember, my father has always fought to push forward my brother and me through so many difficult circumstances. He always put us first and still does – his sons are his life. To this day he continues to teach us how to live and to be good people.

People come to love my father easily and quickly. His friends find in him a motivator that radiates and is bursting with contagious positive energy. His great smile, brilliant personality and good attitude make for happy days and his friends enjoy being by his side.

My father loves to help all people and above all children.

My brother and I are testaments to his daily fight against cancer as these long years have transpired. He has always shown his passion for life; he could have been stricken with pain from the harshness of the strong treatments, but he always showed his strength, positive attitude and smile; this is why I call him the "Iron Fighter". There is nothing that can destroy him. I am sure this book will impact and change the lives of all its readers, because inside there is wisdom and lessons in how to act while facing the challenges of life.

Continue forward, my dear father. Thank you for being such a special person in our lives. I LOVE YOU!


## CARMEN PORTILLO
## ITALY

My dear Carlos, a few lines to tell you of our memory from our trip to North Carolina in 2004 and how you welcomed us with such warmth. I saw a serene family, handsome nephews and above all, very considerate. Although we did not know one another well, because I was very young when you decided to go to the United States and later I to Italy.

To be a parent is not easy, but I can say that I saw Carlos Patiño as a father that gave and continues to give as much as he is able to his children. You demonstrate your great courage with your strength, dignity and desire to live.

A big hug, my dear Carlos, and may God bless you today and always.

## CHARO HERRERA CALLIRGOS
### PERU

My dear Carlos, you always fought so arduously with much caring, enthusiasm and thinking of the future. A big hug from your friends that love you tremendously.

## CHRIS UTHE
## UNITED STATES OF AMERICA

I want to share some thoughts about you during the time we have known each other.

I am a better man, father and person for having met Carlos Patiño. His brilliant smile and warm daily greeting bring a ray of sunshine to my busy life. It only takes spending a few minutes with Carlos to remind me where my real priorities should be, God and family. Carlos has demonstrated incredible physical and mental strength over the years as he battled illnesses. His illness, however, was never a source of focus for Carlos. Instead he showed that his faith, family, and love of his work and community were the things in his life that really mattered. Every person who ever met Carlos was immediately impressed with his positive outlook.

I recall the summer of 2011 when my wife and son came to see me at work one day. They both overheard Carlos greet a few fellow employees and customers as they entered the building during the lunch hour. They did not know who Carlos was at the time but quickly asked me who this positive, energetic and sincere person was. They immediately saw those qualities in Carlos. I was honored to introduce them to the person I call my friend for life.

## CINDY ZULOAGA
## UNITED STATES OF AMERICA

Carlos, you are by far one of the strongest people I have ever known. Watching you go through this journey to battle cancer has shown your true colors. You have such a wonderful spirit and outlook. It seems you never forget the power of laughter and happiness. You seem to care so much about others and their lives, even in the midst of your own plight. You are amazing. As I journey now with Sofie through her cancer and the subsequent treatments, I realize how a positive attitude can affect one's spirit and stability in such an unknown world. You are an inspiration me as a mother and such an inspiration to Sofie. Thank you for sharing your generous spirit, your heartwarming smiles and laughter and your courage with us all.

## DAISY RODRÍGUEZ
## PUERTO RICO

When I first met Carlos, we spoke about life, children and especially our passion to help others. I felt as if I had known Carlos for many years. Through the years I can say that I have never known anyone more caring and giving than he. When I have asked him for help he never said no and always found a way to accommodate my request, especially when it came to helping children in our community. I feel truly blessed to know Carlos and to call him my dear friend.

## DAVID NICOLETTA
## ITALY

I am honored to write something for you. You inspire me and I know that you will inspire all of my friends and others too.

## DAVID E. SHAW
## UNITED STATES OF AMERICA

When I think about words to describe Carlos, they are the following: Warm, friendly, charming, energetic and optimistic and with a great memory.

## DONNA HENRY
## UNITED STATES OF AMERICA

Carlos, you are a very courageous man. I have seen you go through all the treatments for your cancers, and you never let it get you down. I always see a big smile on your face regardless of the outcome. I truly admire you for your determination to get better. Know that you stay in my thoughts and prayers throughout your journey. It has been a blessing to know a person that is so positive.

## ELSIE RODRÍGUEZ
## PUERTO RICO

I see you as a champion! When I worked in Miami I remember you always smiling, with a great attitude and extremely positive. One day you told me that you have cancer and it really surprised me because I always saw you laughing with the joy of life. You are a role model. Good luck, my friend!

## ERIC CASTILLO GARCÍA
## MEXICO

It's been over five years that I have known my good friend, Carlos Patiño. Words cannot describe his personality or express the great qualities of his being; it is impossible to explain them in a few words. I can only summarize them as such: Carlos is a missionary of God. Why, you ask? Because he is a brave person, an honest man, selfless, honorable and caring. He is always ready to help. But above all he is an untiring fighter. He is proud of his roots and Hispanic heritage. I am convinced that Carlos is like an "angel", with the great virtue of being a human, which makes him a true missionary of God. I am fortunate and am very proud to have found his friendship. A hug to my dear friend.

## ERNESTO HUERTO
## PERU

How would I describe Carlos Patiño? As a great friend and a great human being who does not fold to the harsh realities of life. On the contrary, with each obstacle he confronts in his journey, he becomes stronger with a well-tested spirit.

What else can I say about Carlos? He is a charismatic person with an immense desire to live each moment to the fullest. And finally, that it makes me very happy to know he considers me his friend.

## ESTEBAN SANTILLÁN
## ARGENTINA

Carlos Patiño is quite a character. He is a person that leaves an impression. He is a person that does everything with great desire and heart. Carlos is a person that positively influences the lives of many. Carlos gives help and does not expect anything in return. If I have to compare him with someone it would be with a gentleman of medieval times, elegant and a fighter. A fighter that never gives up, a man with which we are rarely gifted in life and some as fortunate as I have the privilege of knowing. It is a blessing from God that he is a part of my life.

## FERNANDO GARZÓN
## ECUADOR

I met Carlos Patiño when I went for a job interview at a nonprofit organization in Winston-Salem, NC. I then moved to this city to work to help the Hispanic community. Thus began my friendship with Carlos because he also wanted to help our community. I realized what a great person Carlos is and there began a great friendship. Since then I have seen how he has work hard and achieved his goals.

He is now well-known, involved and a very important part of the community. I very much admire and respect my friend, Carlos, for his bravery and perseverance to succeed in life and to meet great goals. I thank God that I found the friendship of such a great person.

## FRANCISCO RIZO
## ARGENTINA

As the years pass, I constantly reflect on the successes and failures that I have lived through and have no doubt that if it weren't for certain people, many of the successes would not have been possible. When I think about this, various people come to my mind that have positively influenced my life. Carlos Patiño is one of them. For years I have admired his ability to continue forward and also his great perseverance. Despite not knowing when his pain and anguish will be over, he is able to keep intact his smile and will to live. Many of us should think of developing the ability to persevere, because often we let ourselves give up or become depressed too soon.

Carlos has shown us that you can reach heights that one can only imagine. He has also shown us the bravery to tirelessly fight against his battle with cancer. I wish there were more people of this caliber, with Carlos's mindset that despite one's language or if he is of American culture, one can do what he wants and can succeed. Carlos is a positive influence in my life and a brave man. Carlos Patiño is my great friend.

I thank God for you, my friend.

## GIOVANNI PARADA
## MEXICO

Carlos, your positivism and will to live will never be extinguished by any sickness.

## GRAZZIA MARÍA
## GONZÁLES DE ROZENFELD
## PERU / ISRAEL

It is said that life is a game that we choose to play. The objective is to discover how to balance our desire to receive into a desire to share with others. My Uncle Carlos plays this game of life on another level. He does it with pure and contagious joy, like a kid at a playground. That is how to live and he has shared his wisdom us in his first book: "PASSION FOR LIFE... A message to the willpower".

Thank you so much, Uncle Carlos!

## GUADALUPE RIESS STONESTREET
## MEXICO

To speak of Carlos Patiño is to speak of strength, perseverance, and optimism because he doesn't give in to adversity. He is a small man in stature but has an immense heart. Carlos is a passionate about the Latin culture, a gentleman and respectful friend. Keep fighting for the life you were given and never tire. With love, respect and admiration.

## GUAYO LANATTA
## PERU

To speak of Carlos, whom we affectionately call Carlitos, is to speak of a human being who is very special to all the people that have known him and better yet, interacted with him. The experience of sharing work time with him allowed us get to know the exceptional human being that in each moment gave many lessons of solidarity, sympathy, understanding and selfless friendship. The decency of his actions, the tidiness of his mannerisms and style always showed us that we were with the kind of friend that unintentionally leaves lessons on humanity to those that are around him.

After many years I reconnected with him and he was just as I remembered, showing this time a side of him I had not known, a tireless fighter against a powerful enemy,...: cancer. It has been a fifteen year battle without a hint of defeat. But that is Carlitos, a person with an iron will that again leaves a life lesson. Maybe this is the answer of the Almighty that rewarded this exceptional being for having been so right in his behavior toward others.

A big hug, my good friend Carlitos.

## GUILLERMO CHARÚN
## PERU

Carlos, my dear friend, how could I possibly describe your personality when in truth you are a tapestry of virtues and immensely and blessed with kindness, honesty and ethics. I would say that you are an inspiration born to pursue professional and personal ambitions. You have vigor living day to day; you make the most of the past and let the future come as it may. I learned that although people and their lives change, friends are forever and I appreciate that you are always there.

I have learned from beings friends with Mr. Carlos Patiño Effio that in the end success in life is measured not by what we have achieved, rather by the obstacles that we have faced. Carlos Patiño Effio is an authentic man that smiles, dreams, cries and lives cheerfully and enthusiastically.

## HAROLD JAHNSEN
## PERU

To my "brother" Carlos Patiño Effio...

I met Carlos in the year 1975 when I began working at the Central Mortgage Bank of Peru. At that time, he worked in the Human Resources Department. He was always a gentleman and very attentive. He was always ready to help. During the years I was at the bank I was a witness of his ability to overcome obstacles in his personal life as much as professional. His humanity is reflected in the way he cared for those that went to him for guidance. Carlos was always ready to help anyone with trouble or that needed support.

We reunited in the United States, after many years he is the same self-starting, attentive, friendly and a strong fighter like no one else. Carlos is actually fighting against cancer, a sickness that has been with him for many years. For this reason, my admiration for him is even greater. I admire him because he is a fighter like none other. I admire him because of his commitment to life, his immense love for his family, the respect and the profound esteem he gives his friends. Carlos is a person that is worth imitating. I am proud to have a "brother" like him. He is always and will always be in my thoughts.

## HAZEL PLEASANTS
## UNITED STATES OF AMERICA

In the midst of the adversities of life, it is inspiring to see how strong and positive Carlos has been. He loves helping people. You are always welcomed with a great smile as he shares how God's grace and mercy keeps him motivated.

## HUGO VÁZQUEZ
## URUGUAY

My dear Carlos, thank you for your sincere and selfless friendship, one that endures and strengthens over time. I do not need to see you every day because I know that you will always be there when I need you. Distance, class and culture do not matter; you are always full of affection, courtesy and understanding for all. With love, Hugo.

## INGRID CASSETTA
## GUATEMALA

I send you a few but sincere words.

Carlos is a man that is full of much passion and enthusiasm for life, who never gives no as an answer.

## IRMA TEALDO
## PERU

Carlitos, you are very special to me. I have known you since we lived in Barranco, Lima-Peru. Your parents were marvelous. You were a just and mature person from a young age, polite and sweet. I learned to admire you from Gina, your loving neighbor. She always told me how good you were. I remember well you driving your car, always respectfully saying hi to everyone. My eyes filled with tears when I read of your cancer and with happiness to know you live and with great faith. You are a champion and nothing can or will stand in your way on your journey. You radiate happiness. You have the gift to give love; I can see it in your eyes.

Carlitos, thank you for the giving us the story of your life in your book. Love and peace for you now and always. May God bless you and your family. I love you very much.

JACK BRASWELL
MEMBERS CREDIT UNION / PRESIDENT
UNITED STATES OF AMERICA

Carlos Patiño came to Members Credit Union in 2004. During these 8 years, I have been able to get to know him both professionally and to some degree personally. From the very beginning I have, and do consider, his hallmark strength his extremely positive attitude. It is infectious to all who stand in his presence. As a representative of MCU, Carlos brings a fierce loyalty and all inclusive work style. He is respectful, well-dressed, charming and always friendly. Those who meet him once or time and time again will always receive a genuine smile. Carlos is truly one of a kind. Anyone who gets to know Carlos personally will quickly learn that he has a huge heart, he loves his family, all children and soccer. While he battles some physical challenges, he is a warrior. His mental strength is magnificent and drives him beyond what anyone would expect. I believe my life is exceedingly richer from knowing Carlos Patiño.

## JAMES AND JANE MILANESE
## UNITED STATES OF AMERICA

We met Carlos some years ago at a restaurant in Greensboro, NC. He seemed to know everyone. Before this we had heard of his great love of Americans and his dedication to his work as Director of Latin Services at Members Credit Union.

As he is Peruvian, Carlos has a lively and animated accent, charm and a kind nature. With time, Carlos's friends became our friends. Carlos was an "ambassador of goodwill", with a brilliant smile shining to all.

It was a surprise to know he was fighting against cancer for more than a decade. He never showed negativity. In truth, standing beside Carlos and seeing his positive attitude makes us think about our outlook on life. How can someone be so optimistic, so inspiring and triumphant when he is facing challenges no different than Job, the servant of God faced? I don't know if Job had a good sense of humor, but Carlos definitely does.

Carlos only speaks of his illness when asked. He is a proud man and does not accept pity and does not want others to take on his burden. He only wants your friendship. To be Carlos's friend is a blessing. He is more than a friend; he is a life abundant with knowledge, inspiration, generosity and compassion. He is passionate, generous and caring. He is a father and grandfather, and a man of his word with great goals for his life. The only thing that supersedes his life goals is his integrity. Carlos is very perceptive and can easily understand the character and personalities of others.

I hope Carlos's story positively impacts your lives. After all, he wrote this book to help each of us.

## JASMINE REYES
## DOMINICAN REPUBLIC

Carlos Patiño is undoubtedly an extraordinary human being. I have never seen a person with so much passion for life like Mr. Patiño. No matter what, he is always positive and he never gives up. Even in the worst of times he maintains a positive attitude. He is a Survivor, a fighter and a true warrior. Carlos is an admirable person.

## JASON BROWN
## UNITED STATES OF AMERICA

Carlos Patiño is my good friend, my "Peruvian brother", an incredible fountain of inspiration and example, a person blessed with a positive mind. I envy his boundless energy in the face of adversity. Everyone can learn much from my friend Carlos.

## JEANNIE DUDLEY
## PUERTO RICO

I feel honored to know and have been able to care for Mr. Patiño. His uplifting personality and zest for life are inspiring. Carlos has never let his disease control his life nor attitude. He is an example of mind over matter. He knows how to live his life to the fullest and encourages all of us to do the same. His passion is to live life and he is not afraid to live despite everything he is going through.

Bravo, Carlos!

## JENNIFER NÚÑEZ
## PERU

My dear Carlos, if there is anything that can be said of you it is that your great fighting spirit is worthy of praise and you are undaunted in the face of such a strong sickness that robs so many lives. You have maintained your positive thinking and that has been a great part of your secret to finding victory. Keep it up because I am sure you are a role model for many people that have had lesser challenges than you have had to deal with throughout the years. God bless you.

## JENNY V. MARTÍNEZ
## PERU

I met Carlos while I worked at the place he ate lunch at almost daily. He knows that we are fellow countryman and he offered us a great bond of friendship and confidence. He confronts his battle daily; he would tell me of his joys and sorrows, his work and the weight of responsibility he felt on his shoulders, his great love for his children and grandson; his stories made my respect grow for this man who was always a tireless fighter against adversity.

Professor Freierich of Houston said: "The cancer patient should act like a bullfighter, alone in the square against the bull", and that is what Carlos showed me many times when I asked how he could overcome and smile when things seemed so forlorn. At other times he would arrive happy to have won one of his many daily struggles that he had to face. He really is worth admiration.

## JOHN BARTLETT
## UNITED STATES OF AMERICA

Carlos, you always have a wonderful attitude towards life no matter what your situation is. Your friend, John.

## JORGE AND VICKY GARCÍA
## CUBA

Working at the Cancer Center we have had the wonderful opportunity to meet many people that have impacted our lives in a very positive and memorable way, but none of them quite like you. You are an amazing person that we will carry in our hearts forever. You are an inspiration to everyone, especially those fighting the same battle as you. Your quest for life and external youth are a testament to those that take life for granted. We are very proud to call you our friend.

## JORGE RUIZ
## PERU

I remember the first time I entered the office of Members Credit Union in Winston-Salem, North Carolina, and an elegant gentleman greeted me in a suit and tie, smiling, with an impressive charisma, but above all with an impressive energy that only a sincere person may possess. That is Carlos Patiño. Immediately we spoke and he put things in order. Today we are good friends and I admire all his strength in his fight against cancer, his character and above all his great heart that sees no bad. On the contrary, I think he has the ability to transform the negative into positive.

Go ahead, Carlos. You are admirable, an example with your daily fight and persistent smile. I know that very soon you will regain your health; all of your friends will celebrate with you and will be very proud of all you have accomplished. A big hug, my "brother".

## JOSÉ ROCHEZ
## HONDURAS

It's a true pleasure to greet you again. I hope you have success with your book. As far as I am concerned, for the few minutes I was able to share with you, the truth is that I learned a lot in that short time. I learned how to see life positively and how to be happy with what God has given us without questioning him. I also learned to live day to day with a smile. God bless you.

## JOSÉ VILLAHERMOZA
## VENEZUELA

Simple words for a giant among us! A great inspiration for many people. An untiring fighter.

To you, whom I call friend, with best wishes from all who admire you. God bless you for your dedication to our Hispanic heritage despite your illness. My best regards!

## JOSEPH ANDERSON
## UNITED STATES OF AMERICA

You are a wonderful man, a great friend and an inspiration.

## JOSEPH M. COREY
## UNITED STATES OF AMERICA

My wife and I had the extreme good fortune and pleasure of being a neighbor of Carlos and his family for a year. I was new to Greensboro at the time and found much comfort in being able to develop an immediate friendship with Carlos, in a time when I could really use a friend. He was someone I could talk to about my life, my family, my faith, my business; he was someone I could count on.

It was not long into our friendship that Carlos told me about his misfortunes with his health. At the time he had beat cancer twice. It was important for him to let me know in many ways that it is maintaining a positive attitude that attributed most to his recovery and his happiness with life. His message was simple: always stay positive and never lose faith and you can achieve anything.

Though life has taken us in different directions, I will never forget the times we spent together. His outlook and attitude toward life have been such a positive influence on me. I do my best to try to achieve what my friend Carlos has achieved. I carry the gift of his message with me every day. I think to myself, especially in the tough times, if I can try to achieve the level that Carlos inspires, there is a good chance I can achieve what I set out to achieve, which is anything.

Selfishly for me, knowing Carlos has and will continue to be an extreme benefit to my life. Having been exposed to such a special person who has suffered through so much, who is the epitome of the ideal way to think and live life almost seems unfair. But that is Carlos always giving and never selfish, even if it is his misfortune that is the source. I am a proud friend of Carlos.

## JUAN CARLOS MONCALEANO
## COLOMBIA

Hello my dear friend. Since I met you I've known what a great man you have been, are and continue to be. The truth is I am amazed to see the strength that you have to resist your sickness that has haunted you for so many years and how brave you have been to not let it defeat you. My friend, you are truly an example for us and show us that God is always with us and gives us strength to endure any affliction or hurt. You are a man full of love for your fellow men that continue to carry on your work. Thank you!

I am also proud that you are a Hispanic with courage and have triumphed in both working and humanity in the United States, which gives us confidence that we can all see that it is possible to achieve goals.

I personally wish you success in your life and that you continue forward with the help of God Almighty. Congratulations!

## JUAN PABLO REYES
## ECUADOR

Dear Carlos, is a great pride to have you as my friend. Your strength and courage to face this disease is admirable. You know I always count on me for anything you need. Keep fighting because the great human beings like you always succeed. Best wishes.

## JUAN F. ZULUAGA
## COLOMBIA

I have given much thought to what it is I want to say about my friend Carlos Patiño. Many words can be used to describe this incredible man. Words like courageous, strong, entrepreneur, enthusiastic, happy, skillful, intelligent, driven and humble are the words that come to mind at this moment. Unfortunately, these words fall short in describing this "incredible warrior".

I have met many men in my life that have influenced me; however, few have influenced me in the way that Carlos has. He is the ultimate optimist; he lives life to the fullest. Carlos never gives up and fights for what he wants and believes in. He always greets you with a smile and always cheers you up no matter how bad things are in his life or yours. Carlos has taught me to appreciate what I have and who I am. Also he has taught me to thank the Lord every day for all the blessings he bestows upon me. Most of all, Carlos has taught me the value of having a friend like him in my life. I can truly say that Carlos enriches my life by gracing me with his friendship.

Thank you, Carlos. I feel proud that I have met you. I am honored to be your friend. God bless you!

## JULIO VERNE
## PERU

Since I've known Carlos I have always admired his happy way of greeting and welcoming people, even those he does not know, but his humility makes all feel special. He is an example of kindness that many of us should learn from.

Carlos continues to smile at life, regardless of his daily battle against cancer. This is another example of perseverance and strength. He demonstrates how wonderful it is to live life to the fullest and enjoy every minute and thanking God for all.

You are a fighter and proof that nothing can be an impediment in moving forward in life.

## JULIO CÉSAR
## VILLAVICENCIO CASTELLANOS
## CANADA / PERU

Carlos, the only thing I can say about you is that you were always a fair and sensitive person with an innate sense of friendship. Your lifelong friend, "El gato".

## KARLA MÁRQUEZ
## MEXICO

Thinking of you and how much you mean to me...

**C** aliber..., which is your signature characteristic.

**A** ttitude that is always positive against adversity.

**R** espect and love of life.

**L** iberated from thoughts and ample heart to give and to understand.

**O** bsession with the love in all your actions.

**S** ensibility and compassion, your qualities.

**P** assion and devotion within your heart.
**A** ctions and ability to confront your problems.
**T** enacity and loyalty, innate qualities of yours.
**I** ntelligence and audacity you always demonstrated.
**N** onage and youthful personality. You have a good heart.
**O** pportunity to be a winner, which you already are.

You have touched many people with your bravery and courage. You are a good friend. I think of you often. I love you. Congratulations on your book!

KEVEN CARROLL
UNITED STATES OF AMERICA
I've known Carlos for a number of years. There are many words that come to mind to describe him: positive, personable, passionate, motivated, determined, honorable, caring, funny, to name just a few…

One day while sitting in his office, we were discussing his upcoming chemo treatment which would take place the next week and the word I was looking for hit me: Smile. While talking with Carlos that day, he described what would happen to his body after the next treatment and he was also telling me about the rash that he was getting over from his last treatment. We both discussed how difficult the upcoming treatment was going to be and about that time a customer walked by his office and he yelled out *"Amigo"* with a great big smile. I then knew that was the word to describe him... Whatever is going on with Carlos, he wants to smile. I've sat in his hospital room while he was taking chemo treatments and whenever someone would come into the room, he always smiled and greeted them warmly. I've walked into a local restaurant with him and I felt like I was walking onto the old TV show "Cheers" set as folks would yell out "Carlos" and they too would smile.

Carlos loves life and people. He wants to make people smile back at him. He wants people to have the same zeal for life that he does. I've never known anyone to go through the number of chemo treatments that he has and smile the way he does. Yes, some days his smile is bigger than others. But when you come in contact with him you know that from his hearty he is trying to show you the biggest smile he possibly can. Our world would be a much better place if we too would just smile at one another as Carlos does...

Carlos, my good friend, thank you for your smile.

## LOIDA ROCHA
## NICARAGUA

Dear friend, it has been my pleasure to know you and I am grateful because in my brother's most difficult times, Dr. Moises Rocha, who battled cancer, you cheered him up with love until God took him to his presence.

Carlos is kind, caring and very special to my family and I, more than just a friend. I admire how he has fought cancer for fifteen years. He is a brave man that has faith in God. He continues with such strength that he writes a book, which we anticipate to read about his story of his battle, the battle that we hope he will win.

Many blessings!

## LUIS ASTURIAS
## EL SALVADOR

Carlos is a perfect example for all of us. Carlos never gives up and keeps working hard to achieve his goals in life, despite that horrible disease he has. When I see him at a restaurant, he is always laughing, joking and networking for his job. You would not guess that he has cancer. He inspires me that there is hope for everything in life no matter what problems we are facing.

## LUIS AND SONIA ORTEGA
## NICARAGUA / VENEZUELA

Of course, Mr. Patiño, the battle is incessant against a terrible situation and only you know how to handle it, regardless of the pain it produces and the unhappiness it generates; you have confronted it and carried yourself with cheer, enthusiasm and have not given up. One of your prevailing characteristics is love, that engine that has taken you to where you are today and which you will continue to drive you in your fight for life. We admire you and are proud that you are one of us.

## LUIS PALOMINO
## PERU

I have known many people in my life but honestly have never known a person like you. It is an honor for me and for all of the people that know you to have your friendship. A humble heart only a leader like you could have, and thank you for the daily services you give the Hispanic community so that we may have a better way of life.

Thank you, Carlos, for the unconditional support that you offer to all of Hispanics that need you. You deserve thanks and blessings. You are a champion! Thank you for letting me be your friend.

## MARCELA DAVIS
## ARGENTINA

I have known Carlos since 2002 when I went to Members Credit Union as a member of the institution. Carlos's desk was next to the main door. He always kindly greeted me in English until he discovered I am Argentinean and then spoke Spanish. Ever since, we have not spoken English with one another.

In 2006 I began working for Members Credit Union, at which time Carlos was Director of Latino Services. I remember his dedication to work and how full of energy he was.

In 2008 Carlos was diagnosed with cancer for the fourth time.

Carlos has great strength and has great love for people. He is very popular and loved. All, Americans and Latinos, ask about his health and pray for him. Carlos is an inspiration, a fighter, and is enthusiastic about work and about life. Many times he does not feel well he does not complain and still comes to complete his work even the day after his treatments. I admire him, just as I admire the Latino and U.S. community.

May God bless you and continue to give you strength in your fight against cancer, and may you soon recover your health.

## MARÍA ELENA GARCÍA
### ARGENTINA

I have known Carlos for nearly eight years. My impression of him is that I do not know another person that has fought so hard for his life, and despite his grave health problems continues to work hard and is always looking forward to a better future.

## MARÍA CLARA GIRALDO
## COLOMBIA

Carlos is one of the few people that have touched my life and inspired me to live in a better way. He showed me how to love life without complaining about the small problems that I sometimes encounter. I admire him more than anyone and also admire his passion for life and his strength. Every time I speak with him I tell him how much I appreciate and admire him, because I would not be as strong as him if I had to face all of the obstacles that he has had to live through. I am sure he will be with us for many more years because as he told me: "I will not let sickness take control of my life", and I agree because he is stronger than that.

With love.

## MARÍA DEL MAR HERNÁNDEZ
## COLOMBIA

Carlos, I don't even know where to begin talking about the influence that you have had on me. By fate I have had the pleasant opportunity of recently spending a lot of time with you, and I thank God that He has allowed me to more deeply know the person that never gives up and has shown me to be more grateful with life. Thanks to you I have grown as a person and have learned to appreciate what is truly important in life and to leave aside the petty things, which perhaps I gave too much attention to at some point.

Eyas and I have enjoyed every moment and also the conversations that we have had with you. I want you to know that we admire you intensely. You are an example in our lives, and with God's help we hope to continue counting on your friendship for many more years.

Keep moving forward because with your presence you make the world a better place.

## MARÍA JULIA TELLO
## PERU

Carlos, you are a man with great character, many friends, happy, caring, understanding, social, responsible, respectful, strong and with much love for your family and on top of all you are still so handsome. Carlitos, I pray for you every day with my sister for your full recovery. I know that our Dear God always hears me. I want to be your friend forever. I send a big hug from a great distance.

## MARTÍN BALAREZO GARCÍA
## PERU / UNITED STATES OF AMERICA

My dear friend Carlos, I write to you a few brief words to show my great admiration for your monumental battle for a beautiful life that we all deserve to enjoy. Many times those that enjoy good health do not appreciate it. Each time that we do not enjoy the present is a moment less in our own lives, and one more moment that is thrown into the corner that lacks beautiful memories.

You're a great man because great men are not the tall or big, but those that seek to discover what lies beyond the little world that surrounds us..., and the world waits for you, my friend.

155

You have the courage to fight and the hope to triumph.

I am so proud to be your friend and to participate in the publication of your book, "PASSION FOR LIFE... A message to the willpower", which is laden with emotion and lessons, and allows us to learn of your story that will benefit all. A big hug!

## MARY JANE LANTOR
## UNITED STATES OF AMERICA

Carlos and I started work the same year at Members Credit Union. I remember him speaking with broken English and everyday taking steps to improve his English and making contacts with our members. Occasionally, we would talk and he would say he was Super Charlie. I thought that strange and didn't know why. As time went on his English got much better and he was bringing in many new members and making a name for himself at the credit union. In our conversations the Super Charlie name would still come up. I will say that he is one of the most dedicated, trustworthy, sincere and hardest working people I have ever met. Carlos is also a loving father and grandfather.

All of his accomplishments have been done while fighting cancer, which he has had off and on for years beginning when he was in Miami. As I found out not all that long ago, Carlos is Charlie in English. The name Super Charlie was given to him by his friends in Miami when he beat his cancer the first time. That is a fitting name for him because he is indeed Super Charlie to his family, his friends, his members and to me. He is a great inspiration and a dear friend.


## MAX HINKLE
## UNITED STATES OF AMERICA

I first met Carlos Patiño eight years ago at a restaurant that had just opened for business. Carlos looked like he had just stepped out of the pages of a GQ magazine, acting like he had just won the Power Ball lottery. I thought he must be the owner because of the way in which he was greeting the customers as they walked in and checking to make sure everything was to their satisfaction. It was only later that I discovered that he was only helping his friend get the restaurant up and running.

I had no clue that he had been fighting cancer for seven years and was currently undergoing chemotherapy. Carlos is always in a good mood and he never allows his illness interfere with his ability to be happy and enjoy his friends.

Carlos has been fighting cancer for fifteen years now. We have become very close friends over the years, and I have never met anyone who possesses as positive an attitude as his. I am proud to call him my friend.

## MELANIE HUFFMAN
## UNITED STATES OF AMERICA

When I think of you, I think of someone who is an inspiration to everyone. You truly are an amazing person. You always have a smile on your face and never miss an opportunity to say "hello" to someone passing by your office. No matter how badly you feel (and I know you feel very bad at times) you are always smiling and are of course your friendly, happy self. I remember when I was dealing with the sickness of my father; you would come in my office every chance that you had to ask me how he was. You were concerned about ME and MY FAMILY even with everything you had going on in your life. I honestly believe that you are one of the strongest men that I have ever known. You keep that smile on your face and keep your head up – it's the reason we all know you will beat this! You are a very special person and friend. Thank you for allowing me to be a part of your life. Your American Sister, Melanie.

### MIGUEL R. ESTELLA
### PERU

Hello my dear brother Carlitos.

Congratulations for your book and your accomplishments. You are a very special person, humanitarian, supportive, honest and more. I say this and so do many people that also know you.

We have known each other for many years, and during this time we have enjoyed a cordial friendship and many nights of Peruvian Creole guitar.

Carlitos, from this distance (Lima) I send you a big hug for you and your family. May God bless you. With all my heart, Miguel.

## NELLY MUÑOZ DE GIRALDO
## COLOMBIA

Hello Carlos, you are a role model not only because of what you have achieved in your important work as Director of Latino Services at Members Credit Union, but also because of your integrity and tenacity in your fight and your fearlessness against your sickness. You are worthy of my admiration and the admiration of all that know you. You are a role model. Continue with your positivism and wish to live because that is one of the factors that will help lift you and come out ahead of this difficulty.

God bless you so that you may continue to conquer obstacles and triumph.

## NOLO MARTÍNEZ
## PUERTO RICO

I have rarely known a person like Carlos Patiño Effio. Without Carlos knowing, he has been a great inspiration to my family and me.

Carlos shows how to be a good Hispanic and a better human being. I have never known a person that has more desire to live and to triumph than Carlos. His courage and energy are contagious.

I am a fortunate person because he considers me a friend and colleague. His life story and what he has not yet experienced motivate us all very much.

## PAUL SLUDER
## UNITED STATES OF AMERICA

Carlos is perhaps the gentlest, humblest and most appreciative person I have ever met. He always puts others first and has the power to wear a happy face with a perpetual smile no matter the circumstances…, including a very serious and draining long term illness. It is an honor to call him a friend.

## PIERINA LEVY
## PERU

Carlos is a good friend, a good person with integrity and a great human quality and fighter. That is my dear Carlos.

## PRESTON JAMES
## UNITED STATES OF AMERICA

I was once asked to ride with a customer of BMW. Normal conditions as observed, but with the most untypical of characters. A small framed Hispanic man of middle age encasing a personality of grand stature. There was an inexplicably positive focus that derived from somewhere I'd never been. The day restarted, and I as a humbler man. More than a year has passed and the clock ticks. The ants march and pages are written. What are the things remembered? Fragments of time with those special we encounter. Knowing Carlos adds an open chapter in all of us, of us who are so fortunate to call him a friend.

## RAFAEL CHEPOTE MALATESTA
## PERU

Dedicated to my great friend Carlitos.

I met my dear friend and brother at school in Barranco, Lima. He is a great guy in every sense of the word; humble, straightforward, very kind to his friends and an excellent worker. With his great power he achieved positions in the bank where he worked until he made it to the executive level. He was very loved by his peers.

Carlos lost his daughter and was frustrated and destroyed; regardless, he did not give up.

He worked as a taxi driver to support his children and to survive. He went to the United States with nothing. He started washing plates in a restaurant and from there became the business manager. Cancer found him and he is still fighting against it.

Carlos has great charisma and knows how to reach people. After so much effort and on his own efforts he became Director of Latino Services for a financial institution in North Carolina where he is now he Vice President. With his illness weighing down on him and after his treatments he still goes to work the same day he leaves the hospital.

Carlitos, you have great merit and you are illuminated by God. You are a great man and because of that I believe in you and love you. Forever your friend, Rafo.

## RAÚL BARRETO
### PERU

Carlitos, my darling brother, how wonderful it is to know that you are finishing your book and I hope it is not your last. I pray to God, our Father, that He gives you many more years of life and health now that you have fought so many years against that ruthless sickness. We will continue to pray for you.

Brother Carlos, I swear that it is an honor and a privilege to have a friend like you and I don't know an adjective to use for a man like you that has never surrendered to anything…

You are great, Carlitos!

## REBECA QUIROZ
## MEXICO

One of your qualities that has impacted me most is your great spirit, desire to excel, to live and fight against adversity. I admire you very much and pray to God that he continues to give you the strength to continue on your path. Thank you for simply being you, Carlos Patiño.

## REYNALDO HERNÁNDEZ SOTO
## CUBA

Carlos, I have always thought that nations are preserved or lost in the heart of its men. What great luck Peru and the United States have that you preserve them in yours. I hope your book is received by readers, more than just your heartbreaking story of how you must fight day after day against death, but that they see your story of love with which you live every second of your life. With a warm hug always, Reynaldo.

## RICARDO ALCALDE
## PERU

Brother Carlos, there is no greater satisfaction than for a person to know that the people we love find each day full of faith, persistence and battling adversity. Continue on your beautiful path of success and marvelous spiritual success.

The evil shall be overcome in time by God. To fight positively to live is the life that has the most.

Congratulations on your book. I also wrote one that is a metaphysical compendium: "The pleasure on understanding the spiritual". Always and forever Carlos.

## ROCÍO SEDO-ÁLVAREZ
## PERU

Dear Carlos, I was so happy to see you and really you look great. I can tell you that for me it is a great pleasure to know you and at the same time I admire that we have a patriot that has put the name of our country high and at the same time has not thrown in the towel in the battle against a sickness that has taken so many lives.

My dear Carlos, continue fighting. You are a great role model for all of us. With love, Rocío.

## ROSE M. BALL
## UNITED STATES OF AMERICA

I have known Carlos for four years now. I have never met anyone like him. First of all he is the most charming man you could ever meet. He dresses very classy and his appearance is so polished. He is a real gentleman, very respectful and friendly to everyone. He speaks to all the patients and staff every time he comes to the clinic for treatment. Some days he doesn't feel very well, but he always has an upbeat attitude and is optimistic. God is shining through his eyes. He has fought cancer for so long now and we all hope he continues to do well.

## ROSSMERY ALVARADO
## SPAIN / PERU

My dear cousin, whenever we have had a chance, we have reunited and were so happy. Despite our young age we loved to spend time with our family. I always listened to grandma say how handsome, intelligent and good you are. Of course, the way in which you treated her was unique. She had great reason to say you were her favorite. When you changed cars she was the first to take a ride. I remember how happy that detail made her. I also remember when my mom said that my brother was unemployed and you helped him find a job in a bank of Lima.

You are a selfless person, concerned for others, a great friend and an exemplary son and father. We have been witnesses to your strong fight and your decision to go the United States at age 45 without knowing English in search of a better future for you and your family. That is something to salute!

You always maintain a positive attitude, are happy, entrepreneurial and elegantly dressed, all which has not changed in you. Now, even from a distance, we continue to see the relentless fighter and the success you have achieved. To have you as my cousin is a gift and I am sure that each of your friends would say the same about you. I wish the best for you now and always.

## SABRINA HUDSON
## UNITED STATES OF AMERICA

You are such an inspiration to all you meet. You always have a smile on your face, and you are nice to everyone. It brings me joy every time I see you walk through the door. You are a real breath of fresh air!

## TEODOMIRO SIBAJA
## MEXICO

Carlos is a kind, educated and always smiling friend. We met seven years ago in the Winston-Salem, North Carolina Members Credit Union. He was already Director of Latino Services at Members Credit Union in Winston-Salem, NC and he always guided me toward my best financial decisions.

Carlos is an unconditional friend and I admire him enormously. As many know, Carlos has suffered an illness for nearly fifteen years. An illness, which the mere thought of, terrifies us: cancer.

Carlos, with his faith in God and his fortitude he continues in his fight. Regardless of his pain and suffering, he keeps working to help his community.

Continue "brother", I pray to God that he gives you a miracle cure, that he gives you health in return for what you have suffered and so that you may reach your goals.


## THULIO CORROCHANO PAZOS
### PERU

Your courage and will to fight is what has allowed you to move forward in the difficult battle. Continue forward my dear Carlos. It is my wish. A warm hug, Thulio.


## TOTO RIVA
### PERU

My comment is brotherly and friendly. It encompasses a time in our lives greater than the last fifteen years of your tireless fight that human sickness that is inside of you.

I do not want to think about the patient that will soon be convalescent and finally healthy, by the will of God, but of the time when we shared work, life's ups and downs, friendship which I enjoyed sharing with you.

Carlos you have abundant charisma and charm, which one can see in your pleasant smile and your caring and cordial manner.

In the Central Mortgage Bank of Peru you always had the right words, the correct decisions and the solution to problems.

Continue in your fight in which you will be victorious. God bless and protect you.

VICTORIA N. SCOTT

UNITED STATES OF AMERICA

I first met Carlos at a restaurant in Winston Salem, NC. Although I had become used to having Southern men treat me as a lady, nothing could prepare me for Carlos. It was as though he stepped from a time machine where men bowed from the waist and kissed a woman's hand. At first I thought I was being singled out for his charm; however, over time, I realized Carlos made every woman in his presence feel as though they were a beautiful lady.

My kind regard, Carlos, you are definitely a treasure.

## VILMA EFFIO REYES VDA. DE PATIÑO
## CARLOS'S MOM
## PERU

My dear Carlos, as your mother I am very proud to have a son like you, with an indomitable spirit, fighting with so much bravery, determination, selflessness and decisively against all the hardships that have come in your life.

Congratulations for the wonderful book that you have written, in which you tell of your sufferings and leave us wise lessons and a great example of how to move forward against life's difficulties.

Ever since you were a child you were very kind, caring and concerned about the whole family. As many people have needed your help, you always helped with affection, dedication and human warmth.

Your brothers, "Nana" and I, just like all of your friends, are praying to God, our heavenly Father that you will soon recover your health so that you may enjoy the good and beautiful life that is in store for you. With much love, your mom.

## WILL RICHARDS
## UNITED STATES OF AMERICA

My experiences with Carlos were always a pleasure. Nobody is more cordial and welcoming than Carlos. He likes helping people and he has shown his ability to do so with the circle of people who surround him. Carlos works hard and cares deeply. I admire Carlos for his desire to help his fellow Hispanics, and for his openness to all people from all nationalities. Carlos is a great person!

## WILMER DÍAZ
## HONDURAS

In life there are people that leave an impression on the hearts of others. Carlos Patiño is one of them. From the first time I encountered him he impressed me just by his human nature, professionalism and courtesy. That was through a call that I made from New York to Members Credit Union when I needed financial help. Since that time, our friendship has grown through the years.

They say that one must always confront hard times with a good face. I think that I learned that from Carlos. In each call he has always responded amiably, energetically and very happily. I have not had the pleasure to know him in person but I feel as though I have.

Carlos, thank you for your help and friendship. May God bless you!

# EPILOGUE

The 31st of December 2011 arrived, and although not being used to drinking, at midnight I brought in the New Year with a glass of scotch in hand, and with it my hopes of regaining my health and normalizing my life. I welcomed the year 2012 asking God with devotion, strong feelings and overwhelming emotion, to help me end with this big problem. A new year was beginning and with it my earnest desire to finally be a healthy person, full of love to give, receive and share.

In February I arrived in Lima after fifteen years of absence, enjoying a two-week vacation, where I could see my mom, my Nana, my closest relatives and many friends again. It was summertime in Lima and its southern beaches are full of splendid natural beauty. I took advantage of a short break in between treatments to get away. I felt very happy because days before leaving on my trip I received satisfactory results from my medical examination that indicated that the three stomach tumors were very weak. I still remember when I asked the doctor if I was close to being declared in remission.

Upon returning from my vacation, I continued with what seemed like the end of this dismal story. After several sessions, I went to the hospital for the results of my new tests. I think any person, living with a situation like mine, knowing that the disease was almost at its end, would be full of faith and hope and imbued with the assurance that everything would be like a new dawn in life. To my surprise, the three tumors were back and on top of that, there were two more. I had to start a new fight against five tumors.

After much thought and in my eagerness to "help", I called my doctor and left a message telling him that maybe during my vacation, in my desire to look good, I had exposed myself to too much sun, which in some way could have caused the tumors to return. The doctor told me there was no link to what I do or what I had done, but that everything was really a result of the behavior of my difficult disease. With that I began my thirteenth treatment, which ended in June. On July 30 we would know the state of my health again. Unfortunately, after three days of finishing that treatment, an intense pain in my abdomen took me to the hospital. The cancerous mass had grown pushing against my intestines. I had to be hospitalized due to the emergency situation in which I had gotten into. I was subjected to two terribly strong sessions, after which the results of this new attempt would be analyzed. Once again the bad news…: Despite the strong sessions, four of the five tumors had joined to form one large tumor and the fifth had become a second smaller one, and therefore it remained a critical situation.

In early August, I began a new treatment, the fourteenth in the list of hopeful attempts, hoping that it would help me. The day of the second session, my doctor informed me of a new study to provide experimental treatments for patients with advanced hematological malignancies, which has given encouraging results in some cases. I made the decision to participate in that study that I began at the end of August, which unfortunately did not work.

The fifteenth treatment ended in September without the expected results. Despite this I still look forward to being able to end with this torment of my life.

As always, I am still full of enthusiasm and faith, "vitality and energy", and trying to keep my life as normal as possible, working and full of ideas for the future.

I wrote this book with great effort and with love, many times suffering the ravages of the terrible treatments. I couldn't allow myself to interrupt the writing of it because I felt an immense responsibility toward others and the deepest desire for many people to benefit by reading it. It has been a year and a half of total commitment and dedication. Finally, and in the most humble manner, I hope that "PASSION

FOR LIFE... A message to the willpower" impacts and positively affects your life, helps you overcome your problems of any kind and frees you from your limitations. Those are my sincere desires for you, your family, your friends and all who wish to read it.

Your friend, Carlos 😊